BECOME LOADED FOR LIFE!

Financial Independence

Retiring Early

Maximizing Happiness

by Nate Carter

ISBN 978-1-7340107-1-8

CONTENTS

ABOUT THIS BOOK

At the age of 27 I created a plan that turned $1,500 and a $24,000 annual salary into becoming financially independent in 12 years. Instead of losing everything in the 2007-2008 global financial crisis, the worst recession in 70 years, I doubled my net worth. I will show you exactly how I did it. If you read these chapters and complete the corresponding list of tasks in the *Become Loaded for Life! 10 Stages Workbook* you can follow the same exact process. This book is designed to provide you with the skills and the right mindset for creating wealth, becoming financially independent and maximizing your long-term happiness. This is not a passive process; your success requires effort and due diligence, but it is not nearly as hard as you might think.

This book will help you climb out of debt, but that is only the start. My goal is to help you keep climbing to achieve real wealth. I hope to challenge commonly held beliefs about work and education and change the way you view money and spending. We will jettison the traditional plan of working hard for someone else and then retiring at the age of 70 or older.

We will redefine your notions of risk. You will view relying on a job as your sole source of income as incredibly risky, even though this is the path most people are taught to follow. You will realize a job alone is unlikely to make you wealthy even if it pays well. You will learn to stop trading your time for money by creating passive income. We will explore strategies to live below your means in order to invest for a richer, more fulfilling life. We will examine worrying long-term economic trends that could lead to higher taxes and the loss of public retirement benefits. We will also discuss ways to insulate yourself from recessions and job loss.

You will learn about a range of investments to create income streams to reduce your dependency on a traditional paycheck. You will be given the tools to write a plan for financial freedom, *as you define it!* You will benefit most from this approach if you start at a younger age, but it is never too late to begin. Even if you are just a few years away from retirement, this book can help you accelerate your goals and design a more durable retirement.

The first step in this process is to get a copy of the *10 Stages Workbook* available on the website www.LoadedforLife.com. The *10 Stages Workbook* will guide you through specific action steps to create your plan for financial independence. It will become your road map. In the coming weeks and months, you will complete a series of tasks. As you check off each task, you will watch your progress unfold. These tasks are not just about money, they are about creating positive habits related to health, a proper mindset and accountability. Some tasks are minor tweaks to your daily routine which, compounded over time, will bring powerful and lasting benefits. If you complete the *10 Stages Workbook* you should attain financial independence and end your dependence on a full-time job. You should no longer live paycheck to paycheck, you should no longer feel trapped by debt, and you should alleviate money related stress from your daily life. If this sounds like a better way to live, then let's get started.

INTRODUCTION

Defining Loaded for Life

As we begin, it will help to define what I mean by the phrase Become Loaded for Life. It is *living a life of financial independence with adequate resources to pursue life's passions and creating a future with less stress and more opportunity for you and your family.* It is about more than just money. It is about thinking through a set of long-term goals, checking off each achievement, and creating a plan that will lead to a more satisfying life. It is a process that takes you from talking or dreaming to implementing with measurable and sustainable results.

Buckle Up, Savings Rates Are Scary

The current financial situation for average families is truly scary. In the United States 57% of households have less than $1,000 in their savings account and the average household has nearly $16,000 in credit card debt. A Federal Reserve report found 41% of households could not cover a $400 emergency expense and would need to rely on borrowing or selling something to come up with this money. Do you fall into this category? Could you pay a $400 bill that appeared tomorrow? If not, don't worry, because you will learn how to manage a $400 emergency or a $5,000 emergency without having to rely on high-interest credit cards or payday loans.

Retirement Savings Crisis

As a society we are wholly unprepared for the cost of retirement. This is not just within the United States, but in many countries across the world. According to a study by the U.S. Government Accountability Office (GAO), nearly 29% of households age 55 and older have no retirement savings, including pensions. These are people on the cusp of retirement with little time to make up for their lack of savings. Financial advisors increasingly tell their clients to work into their mid to late seventies because they cannot afford to retire. The Economic Policy Institute reports that the average retirement savings of all working-age families is $95,776. However, this figure is misleading because there are a smaller number of families who are aggressive savers, who have portfolios well above this amount, while most families have saved far less than this average. The median amount the average family has saved for retirement is $5,000. A sum of $5,000 could finance a few months of retirement at best. These numbers are frightening, and hopefully they will motivate you to act.

In these pages you will be shown how to become one of these aggressive savers. Some people dream of being able to retire at the age of 65 or 70; my goal is to help you retire decades earlier, and in a way that insulates you from job layoffs and rising health care costs. You will create a plan that fits your budget and is diversified enough to protect you when the economy is in recession.

Money and Stress

A survey by the American Psychological Association found that 72% of adults regularly worry about a lack of money and this worry is a major source of stress in their lives. It is also worth noting that money troubles (after infidelity) are the second leading cause of divorce. For many people there appears to be something fundamentally wrong with their understanding and relationship with money. There are certainly families facing unique financial challenges brought on by a catastrophic medical event or tragic personal loss. However, I am not talking about a limited number of families in extreme situations; statistics show that most working families are facing significant stress and financial strain.

Living Paycheck to Paycheck

More than 59% of workers are living paycheck to paycheck. Referring again to the Federal Reserve report, 27% of respondents said they skipped medical treatments in the past year due to the cost of treatment, while 22% said they expect to forgo payments on some of their bills during the month. Not paying a bill or making partial payments will damage your credit score which will create more money problems in the future. Nearly 12 million people rely on high interest payday loans to make ends meet. Surprisingly even people with well-paying jobs fall within these troubling statistics and are worried about money. *The problem is frequently not the size of a person's paycheck, it is how they spend and their lack of understanding about how money works.* Money is merely a tool and you have to learn how it works to take advantage of it.

As you read this book and complete the workbook you will see how to avoid living paycheck to paycheck, regardless of your current income level. You will learn how to track and control your spending, form habits that create wealth and most importantly, set yourself on a path to maximize your happiness.

A Newspaper Route and a Recession

My interest in personal finance and entrepreneurship started when I was a kid in Chicago in the 1980s. I tried dozens of little enterprises including shoveling driveways in the winter and selling products door to door in the summer. I also picked up a newspaper route which taught me two valuable lessons about money and its correlation to happiness.

While delivering newspapers, I noticed that people frequently threw items away that were still in working condition or only needed a simple repair. I collected these items and stored them in my garage. I was not sure what to do with them, but I disliked seeing things of value go to waste. I soon realized I could sell everything I collected in a big garage sale. Since I paid nothing for these items, every dollar was pure profit. I made $200 from my first garage sale, which was more than I earned from my newspaper route in four months. This was the first lesson; keep an eye out for financial opportunities because they are all around you. I had leveraged my low paying newspaper route into a far more profitable garage sale business.

My newspaper route years also coincided with the 1980-82 recessions, providing the second important lesson, that relying on a job as the sole source of income was very risky. In recessions employment becomes fragile and the loss of a paycheck can have a dire impact on family stability and happiness. As the recession wore on, emerging into two recessions in close succession, some of the parents on my route lost their jobs and were forced to move. The uprooting of families and stress led to an increase in the number of divorces in our neighborhood. I was eleven years old, but the experience has been an indelible reminder to create multiple income streams and to have emergency funds to weather economic downturns.

Taking Quitting Off the Table

In my twenties my entrepreneurial interests took a backseat to a desire to see the world and give back to society. I joined the U.S. Peace Corps and served in Africa for 27 months. I learned what most people would expect from this type of experience, coping without creature comforts and navigating a country that is quite different from my own. It was a rewarding experience, but was also remarkably challenging, which led some volunteers to resign and return home.

I decided early in my tour that no matter the level of hardship, I would complete my full term of service. I call this *taking quitting off the table*. The decision was instantly freeing. As I hit low points, I worked to overcome the challenge and lift my spirits, but I knew quitting was not an option. This was a tremendous lesson in patience and persistence and has served me well ever since. If you set your mind to a goal and take quitting off the table you will succeed, whether it is to be a millionaire, to visit every country in the world, or to retire when you are 40 years old. *Nothing clarifies the mind like the absence of alternatives.*

Many Peace Corps Volunteers, like the communities they live with, do not have running water or electricity. They live in mud houses and experience an entire range of illnesses. As you adapt to this life you learn the necessity of negotiating for ten minutes to save 20 cents on a bag of vegetables, and you learn to avoid the meat at the butchers without flies, because it was sprayed with pesticide. Africa was an amazing experience, but I also saw the challenges locals faced to get ahead financially or to launch a business. It all seemed infinitely more difficult than it would have been in the United States with a regularized system of enforceable contracts, access to credit, and clearly defined property rights. Seeing these obstacles made me truly appreciate the gift of being born in a country that allows its citizens the opportunity to climb the economic ladder. It may not be easy, and we each may be starting off at a different rung, but a path exists if you are willing to put in the effort to make the climb.

When I finished my service, I felt like a new immigrant coming to America seeking to make my fortune. I moved to Washington D.C., found a small basement apartment with security bars on the windows and I landed a job making $24,000 a year. I was 27 years old, had $1,500 to my name, and knew nothing about investing.

I also had a sense of unease as I was financially way behind friends who were a few years into their careers. A healthy amount of fear can be a great motivator, and I used it to rapidly educate myself. I spent nights and weekends learning the difference between stocks, bonds, IRAs, index funds, REITS, and eventually rental properties. I read every book I could get my hands on at the library. I also spent hours online learning about various aspects of business and investing.

Designing a Financial Life Plan

During this research I learned that the medical device company Medtronic writes a 100-year strategic plan to chart its future. I thought if a company has a 100-year plan, then clearly, I should have a 30-year strategic plan. I discussed this idea with Sarah, my then girlfriend and now wife, as we mapped our shared goals. We wanted a simple plan to guide our future, something that could be flexible but get us to where we hoped to be one day. The result was the five bullets below:

• We identified how much passive income we would need coming in each year to cover all our expenses and to become financially independent. I then calculated how much we needed to save in a portfolio of investments to provide this income. The goal was to eliminate the need for two full-time jobs. *We did not necessarily want to stop working; we wanted to be able to stop working.* My calculations said we could save this nest egg and quit working in 30 years when I was 57 years old. We thought a 30-year plan seemed manageable, but as you will see, we reached our goal in less than 12 years.

• Second, our goal was to ensure that our passive income would be enough to allow us to maintain our current lifestyle. We did not want to retire into austerity. We would track our annual spending and look for ways to cut unnecessary expenses. As you cut spending, you can reach your target faster.

• Third, we factored in risks such as future recessions, higher taxes, or reductions in government benefits like Social Security. You must anticipate these downside risks into your planning if you want your plan to be durable and protect you from painful decisions in the future. The 1980-82 recessions were still forefront in my mind and our plan had to be able to weather such downturns. This approach helped us successfully navigate the global financial crisis and should guide us through the next major recession.

• Fourth, we hoped to spend a decade or more living overseas exploring the world. Your plan should not be limited to finances, it should define how you wish to spend your lives along the way. We also wanted to travel light by focusing more on experiences than acquiring possessions.

• Fifth, we wanted to have a healthy work/life balance. The world is beginning to recognize how truly damaging years of sustained stress can be on your long-term health. We were not willing to trade a high salary for 80-hour work weeks. You will soon learn in these pages that the hourly returns on those jobs can actually be much lower than less stressful jobs due to taxes and required expenses.

CHAPTER 1: IMPLEMENTING THE PLAN

This was our whole plan, five simple bullets to keep us focused. In the first few years our salaries were modest, but they grew over time. We both brought our lunch from home each day to save on food costs, walked or biked to work to save on transportation costs, and only went out to dinner for special occasions. We looked for creative ways to reduce our entertainment expenses and took advantage of the extensive free museums and cultural events in Washington D.C. Strategies for saving like this will be explained in greater detail later. We also contributed the maximum amount to our employer's retirement plans and turned our attention to learning more about real estate.

Real Estate and Taxes

We spent many weekends going to open houses to teach ourselves about the local real estate market, which was both educational and fun. Within a few months we could guess a house's list price to within $2,000 just by walking through it. After analyzing 75-100 houses in our market, we knew when we found an underpriced property. This was before Sarah and I were married, and we decided to make our first real estate investments on our own.

I bought a $123,000 two-bedroom apartment as my primary residence with a down payment of 10%. I immediately found a roommate which reduced my housing expenses by more than half. *This one decision of getting a roommate to pay most of the mortgage was a game changer financially.* Soon after, Sarah bought a studio apartment for $50,000, using a 10% down payment of $5,000. I had discovered a new first-time homebuyer's tax deduction that paid her back the full $5,000 down payment.

This allowed her to buy the property for only $2,500 in closing costs. *We quickly realized how much it pays to learn about taxes, particularly for real estate.*

After we got married, Sarah's apartment became our first rental property as she moved in with me. We choose to rent our properties at slightly below market rates to appeal to a wider pool of qualified applicants. We have found this strategy increases our rents in the long run through lower vacancies and having happy tenants who know they are paying below market rents.

Trading Lunches for a Property

A year later we purchased another studio apartment for $68,000 with a 10% down payment. We used the $5,000 tax refund from Sarah's apartment to cover most of the down payment. We only had to pay about $4,000 to cover the rest of the down payment and closing costs. *By bringing our lunches to work for two years we saved the $4,000 to buy this property; lunches for a condo is a pretty amazing trade. It was also a valuable lesson in putting our money to its best use.* We later converted this studio apartment into a one-bedroom which significantly increased its value and allowed us to raise the rent. There are tremendous benefits to forcing appreciation by modifying or fixing up a property. Along with the savings from tax incentives and the regular rental income we realized how important real estate is to creating wealth and financial freedom. *Real estate needs to be one of the key components of your financial plan.*

Within a year, the two investment apartments were generating about $400 in monthly cash flow. This $400 per month was our first income stream outside of our regular jobs. The rental properties and taking on a roommate in my first property showed us how to lower our housing costs and create income streams that could eventually replace our jobs. *Each dollar you earn from an investment replaces a dollar that you need to earn from a job. In addition, every dollar of your expenses that you cut provides another dollar to invest, thus accelerating the process of wealth creation.*

Trust Your Gut and Your Numbers

Within a few years real estate prices had climbed dramatically and we could not find properties that would yield a monthly profit. I will explain the calculations we used in the sections on real estate. Buyers were also waiving home inspections which we thought was risky. Without an inspection you don't know what might be wrong with the house. In response, we stopped buying real estate. *This is a lesson worth remembering, if your calculations indicate real estate is no longer profitable and buyers are waving home inspections you are probably in a real estate bubble and need to proceed with caution.*

Interestingly, the advice we were given at the time was not to worry. We were told real estate will continue to go up in value and investors will profit from the appreciation. This was the early stages of the emerging global financial crisis. By trusting our gut and our calculations we protected ourselves from over-paying for real estate. We also sold two of our properties at a significant profit. I like the recommendation we have since heard, *"if you won't buy at these prices, you might want to sell at them."* We avoided the worst of the financial crash that would eventually come, and we had the profits from the sales to buy real estate after prices had fallen dramatically. Being cautious and filtering out the real estate hype allowed us to accelerate our plan instead of watching it crumble.

As real estate prices fell, we watched as other investors, who overpaid for multiple properties, were forced to sell at a discount. *This was another important lesson in real estate investing; you only lose money if you must sell.* If you can weather the storm, the value of your investments should recover. Buying at the right price and minimizing your exposure to excessive debt is how you protect yourself from having to sell.

Buy Your Retirement Home Today

Investing in real estate showed us how we could use the rent from tenants to pay off a mortgage. With this in mind, we decided to buy our retirement home now and let our tenants pay it off over the next 15-20 years. We were not certain where we wanted to retire, but we had a few cities in mind. We looked for areas where real estate had not become too overvalued. We took long weekends visiting other states to look for properties. Once you know the basics of how to buy a property, it becomes easier to invest out of state. We decided on a city and bought our retirement home during a visit. By renting out this property over the years we now have a paid off retirement home.

Chasing the Next Life Goal

By this time, we were ready to leave Washington D.C., and wanted to pursue our goal of living overseas. We both took a pay cut of nearly 20% for jobs that would take us to the Middle East. Even though our salaries were lower, our living expenses declined because our employer provided housing, thus eliminating our housing costs which for most people is their largest monthly expense. Remember, your plan is not only about increasing your salary; it is often worth taking a lower paying job if there are other nonmonetary benefits or if it will help you achieve other major life goals.

Saving on State Income Taxes

By changing jobs, we were no longer tied to Washington area and could re-establish our home base anywhere we wanted. We rented out our apartment, we were already renting out our future retirement home, and we decided to buy a property that would be our primary residence. We visited various cities and bought a property in a less expensive city which happened to be in a state with no income tax. We immediately saw a significant increase in our after-tax income from this move. The savings on state income tax paid a significant portion of our new mortgage. This was another great lesson on the value of living in an area with a lower cost of living, particularly low taxes.

Living Below Your Means

For the next few years we remained overseas, living below our means. If we got a raise, we would immediately invest it, remaining at our previous standard of living. This helped us to save, pay down our mortgages, and make other investments. We maximized our contributions to our employer retirement accounts, which are primarily invested in an S&P 500 stock index fund. During the global financial crisis, we invested more aggressively when others were looking to get their money out. We stayed committed to our plan while recognizing how fortunate we both were to retain our jobs during the recession.

Completing a 30-Year Plan in 12 Years

Everything we learned along the way is explained in these pages. The steps we followed are listed as specific tasks in the *10 Stages Workbook* available at LoadedforLife.com. There is a condensed version of the specific tasks in appendix 2, but to truly understand the process please go through the workbook. By completing these tasks, we hit our original 30-year target in 12 years, trimming 18 years from our timeline. We had also fulfilled our plan of living overseas including in Syria, Lebanon, Uganda, and Jamaica. We decided to have a family and now had two boys joining us on our adventure.

Reassessing and Setting New Goals

Once we achieved our original financial goal, we took some time to reassess our position and our future. We knew we would need some additional resources to cover the added expense of raising two kids. We also became increasingly concerned about long term health care costs and thought we should save more for health-related expenses. We had reached a point where we could change careers, take some significant time off or only work part-time. Neither of us wanted to quit working as we generally liked our work. All jobs have daily ups and downs but ours offered the option to remain overseas which is what we really wanted. We chose to keep working and challenged ourselves to see how long it would take for us to double our net worth.

Diversifying Investments Based on Time Commitments

We continued to maximize contributions to our employer retirement plans and put money into a range of different types of investments all of which are described in the following chapters. We also learned a valuable lesson about investments and time commitments. *Each investment takes a certain amount of your time to manage and just as we diversified for risk, we also learned to diversify our investments based on the required time commitment.* Investments such as renovating properties to turn them into rentals are time intensive, while other investments such as purchasing index funds of stocks require nearly no time at all. As you create your plan for financial freedom, look to diversify your investments based on asset class and the required time commitments.

Second Goal Reached in Eight Years

By using what we learned in the first twelve years we were able to reach our new financial goal in eight years. Our ability to weather the worst financial crisis since the Great Depression and still double our net worth is a testament to creating a plan and sticking to it. During those eight years we lived in the United Arab Emirates, Fiji, and New Zealand. We have been fortunate enough to visit nearly 70 countries including some of the more remote corners of the world. Not everything went perfectly, there were numerous challenges and mistakes along the way, but in total the plan worked exceedingly well.

Our goals focused on travel and living overseas, *but this is not a book about achieving our goals. It is a book to help you achieve your goals.* Your plan will be different and will reflect your dreams and ambitions. Maybe you want to be debt free and one day pay cash for a Tesla. Or spend your days fishing by a lake or skiing all winter. Maybe you want to pay off your home in 10 years or pay for your kid's college without debt. Perhaps your goal is simply to never worry about money ever again. Creating these choices for yourself and your family is empowering. You define the goals and whatever they might be; following the lessons in this book and specific tasks in the *10 Stages Workbook* will help you get there.

Personalize Your Plan to Become Loaded for Life!

Since you are the architect of your plan, it will be unique to your specific needs and targets. Although a primary goal may be quitting the rat race to focus on work you truly enjoy, your goals should be about more than just quitting work. You want to work towards something positive not just seeking to leave something negative. As part of this process you must also assess your tolerance for risk. You might be comfortable retiring with a modest income stream that just covers your basic expenses (food, shelter, utilities) while finding short-term work to supplement your income as needed. Other people want a wide moat of financial protection, taking comfort in knowing they will never need to work again. Know where you fall on this spectrum as you design your plan.

As part of the interactive approach to this book, you need to go to LoadedforLife.com and get a copy of the *10 Stages Workbook* if you have not already done so. Once you buy the workbook, take a few minutes to reflect and write down four or five goals you have for yourself. What do you want your life to look like over the next ten years? As you read these pages, make no mistake, you are at a crossroads and the decisions you make will define your future. If you stay the course of reading this book and diligently complete the workbook tasks you will see these four or five goals come within your grasp. As you stay the course you will achieve all of them and much more.

CHAPTER 2: CHANGING YOUR MONEY MINDSET

This chapter delves into creating the right mindset for fostering wealth creation and teaches you to re-evaluate your perceptions about money and millionaires. We also look at approaches to spending money and avoiding common traps that lead to spending on the wrong things.

Responding to Opportunity

When we first started implementing our plan, I discovered a $5,000 tax credit for first-time home buyers. We used this credit to recoup 100% of our $5,000 down payment on a property. When I first learned about the tax credit, I felt like I had struck gold. In my enthusiasm I told a colleague, who was at my same income level, about the tax credit. I assumed this person would say, "Wow that is amazing! I need to use that too!" The actual response was *"Yeah, they don't want you to know about that."* This surprising response and the negative reaction to a valuable opportunity has stuck with me ever since.

I could not fathom what this person meant. Who does not want you to know about it? The tax credit is public information, the government clearly wants people to use it to help revitalize a struggling real estate sector. The more I thought about this comment, it sunk in how much wealth creation is a mindset. Your ability to create wealth is a result of how you see the world. Do you believe that one person's gain is another person's loss? Do you believe that money is scarce and hard to obtain? Or do you believe that money is abundant, and you will become wealthy if you are determined to make it happen?

Pause and think for a moment how you would respond in this same situation of being shown a $5,000 tax credit for purchasing a property. Would you see a great new opportunity? Or would you find an excuse not to take advantage of it? Honestly answering this question will tell you a lot about your money mindset and how much you may need to change it.

I would never assume that everyone in life has the same talents, abilities, or opportunities. But in life you must make your luck. If you think the world is against you and believe the reason you will not become wealthy is because the system is against you, then your greatest obstacle to success is self-imposed. If you see the world with this negative view you need to work to revise it, opportunities exist all around us and the right mindset is how we learn to seize them.

Money May Not Buy Happiness, But It Provides Well Being

How you define happiness depends on what personally brings you joy, but for all of us a fundamental way to create a sense of security and wellbeing is to remove money related stress. Financial insecurity is a key contributing factor to high rates of divorce, depression and, tragically, many suicides. It is also a key factor in couples choosing not to have children. As you create multiple streams of income, you will notice how it insulates you from such stress. You become less concerned about losing your job, or a downturn in the economy, or a bad year in the stock market because these negative events are less of a threat to you and your family.

The right mindset, and the corresponding wealth it brings, means you will not be afraid that you can't afford to make a major repair to your house or pay for a necessary medical treatment. As these expenses emerge, you can calmly absorb them without resorting to credit cards or making painful sacrifices in other areas of your life. That is the benefit of the strategies in this book. It requires a change in mindset and some tough decisions in the first few years, but you soon become insulated from most issues related to money. You can then focus your energy on the more positive and productive aspects of life.

Money is Not Evil

Many people have a strange and sometimes unhealthy relationship with money. Money is sometimes afforded mythical powers such as being the root of all evil. This is ridiculous when you recognize that money is simply a tool to facilitate the trade of goods and services. Excessive greed may lead to malevolent actions, but there is no reason to blame money for human emotions or shortcomings.

Similarly, our psychological makeup and brain physiology (responses to dopamine and serotonin) can play an instrumental role in our habits related to saving and spending. We will look at ways to retrain your brain to strengthen your mental fortitude and foster more positive and productive interactions with money. The initial step is learning to view money simply as the tool that it is. Then as you learn how this tool works you can better understand how to use it to your advantage and to achieve your goals.

Millionaires are Not the Enemy, 80% are Self-Made

There are some concerning economic trends related to the rising gap of inequality, our rapidly increasing national debt, the shrinking middle class, excessive worker to CEO pay ratios and stagnant wages in certain occupations. These are issues that need to be addressed to foster longer term economic and social stability. However, there are two key messages to remember as you filter through the news on these types of issues.

First, there is probably no better time in history to start your own business, create a new life for yourself, or take the opportunity for second chances to create wealth. Will this be easy? No, it will take time and dedication. You also can't allow quitting to be an option. But *it is possible* and that should be a key driver in your mind. Being a millionaire or a multimillionaire is 100% obtainable. The more you remind yourself of this fact, the more likely you are to make it happen.

Second, 80% of millionaires in the United States are self-made. This is also the case for millionaires in many other countries as well. According to the book The Millionaire Next Door: The Surprising Secrets of America's Wealthy, only 20% of millionaires inherited their wealth. The other 80% of millionaires are people who created an idea to solve a problem and turned it into a business. Or they are someone who lives below their means, regularly invests, and creates a portfolio worth seven figures. Some people who never earn more than a modest income but were diligent savers are now millionaires. Their success is no reason for animosity; it should spark a desire to create your own path to similar wealth.

It is important to recognize that most people you see driving expensive cars and living in big houses are probably not millionaires. Often, they are living on credit cards and borrowed money. These seemingly wealthy people are a paycheck or two away from losing everything. Studies show that most millionaires live well below their means, own a modest house and drive an average car. These people are the real millionaires, but you would never know it by looking at them.

Money Does Not Buy Status

It remains a mystery to me why so many people seek to acquire things to create happiness or project status to those around them. Studies have proven that trying to validate yourself by comparing your financial situation to others usually results in being less satisfied. Trying to keep up with your neighbors by acquiring luxury trinkets in an effort to convey a certain level of economic status is a fool's pursuit. Do not fall for the sales tactics of advertisers because no type of watch, or clothes, or car makes you smarter or better than other people. Most current and future millionaires do not succumb to this marketing; they are smarter with their money and you should be as well. Time is the greatest luxury, and the way to get more of it is to earn as much as you can and live on the least amount you need. You want to measure your progress, but only against yourself and your goals, not against the living standards of your neighbors.

"See the world. It is more fantastic than any dream made or paid for in factories..." -Fahrenheit 451 by Ray Bradbury

Choose Experiences Instead of Things

A Cornell University study found that paying for experiences like travel or music events have a greater and longer lasting impact on your happiness than the purchase of material goods. I think about this when I see people spend $50,000 to buy a nice car on credit. There are some significant opportunity costs associated with this decision. If you spent $10,000 on a used car you could spend the remaining $40,000 having five life changing experiences such as learning Spanish in South America, taking guitar lessons in Memphis, studying martial arts in Brazil, hiking the Appalachian Trail, or helping rebuild hurricane damaged homes with a humanitarian organization. Unlike new cars or other items that quickly depreciate, these experiences provide skills, contacts and memories that pay dividends for life.

As an example, when we were living in Uganda, we spent $1,500 to travel to Rwanda and volunteered to spend a day painting and fixing up an orphanage. Once we arrived, we learned the event was organized by the humanitarian and author Rosamond Carr. Carr had a fascinating life running pyrethrum farms in Africa. She was a close friend of primatologist and conservationist Dian Fossey, featured in the movie *Gorillas in the Mist*. It was an amazing day of making repairs and hearing about her incredible life. I can't imagine another way of spending $1,500 that would provide such a rich and rewarding experience.

Rent Luxury, Don't Buy It

When it comes to luxury items, it is financially preferable to rent than to own. Renting a boat or a sports car provides the experience without the rapid depreciation and the continued maintenance costs. The excitement derived from luxury items tends to fade quickly as your mind moves on to the next shiny object. If you are absolutely determined to buy that Porsche, BMW or restored 1977 Trans Am you always wanted, I suggest waiting until you reach financial independence.

Once financially free, you can channel all your energies towards this acquisition and you can rely on your passive income to help pay for it. You may also find a way to get the car at a discount or through a creative trade. There is nothing wrong with rewarding yourself; it is one of the benefits of achieving your goals, just make sure the decision is well thought out. Especially if you are thinking about the Trans Am.

The Right Mindset is the Foundation

As you think about your own money mindset and how you may want to revise it, remember that the right mindset is crucial for success. Objectively look at how you respond to opportunities to see if you are open minded or too quick to dismiss them. Do you talk yourself out of potential victories? Try to identify what might be holding you back and consider what you can do to make changes and curb these limitations. You are literally re-training your brain to understand money and potential opportunities, so this will take some time and effort.

Finding people who are also focused on maintaining a positive mindset is an important first step. Surrounding yourself with other positively motivated people provides a valuable support network. Do not try to rush this process. Take your time to think and make notes on areas you hope to change. Write down the money mindset you hope to have and how you plan to get there. Establishing the right mindset cannot be overlooked as it is the foundation for your entire plan.

Key Takeaways:

• Creating wealth and financial independence may require a change in your mindset and perceptions about money. Money is a tool that works to your advantage if you understand it. You control money, it does not control you. Changing your mindset requires a frank assessment of how you perceive both money and wealth, as well as how you respond to new opportunities that present themselves.

• Money is not evil, nor is being a millionaire. More than 80% of millionaires are self-made and did not inherit their wealth. The real millionaires are usually hiding in plain sight, driving older vehicles and living in modest homes.

• Many people who appear wealthy are not; they do not own real assets and are living on borrowed money to support a life-style they cannot afford. Purchasing things will not bring happiness and luxury items are usually better to rent than to own. Spending money on experiences is more fulfilling than spending on things.

• Be honest with yourself about how you need to change your mindset as it will be the foundation for your future success. Begin looking for positive people who are like minded who can be part of your network.

CHAPTER 3: CURIOSITY, MOTIVATION, AND ADVICE

A successful journey to financial independence requires intellectual curiosity, a continuous pursuit of knowledge and sustained self-motivation. You can only get better and grow if you improve upon what you already know. And what you know today will not get you where you hope to be three to five years from now. You need to continuously increase your knowledge. You also need to reexamine the traditional advice of study hard and get a good job, because *on its own* this method rarely leads to financial freedom. And when it does, it usually takes far too long.

The good news is a significant amount of the knowledge you need is free or inexpensive, available in books, articles, videos and podcasts on creating wealth, buying real estate and investing. Try to improve your skills each day by obtaining at least one new piece of information that will help you in revising or implementing your plan. Collect this information in a notebook or electronic document so you can easily refer to it on a regular basis.

"Chance Favors the Prepared Mind" - Louis Pasteur

A great example of always remaining curious regardless of where you are in your life comes from an interview by Guy Raz with Daymond John, the founder of FUBU (For Us By Us) and one of the investors on the television show Shark Tank. John described the challenging early years of building his company when he worked as a waiter at the restaurant Red Lobster. What set John apart from his peers was that he read Red Lobster's quarterly reports and profit and loss statements to understand what made the business profitable.

Raz commented that most waiters don't read their restaurant's quarterly reports. John responded that what they did is not his problem; he was reading them and used the knowledge to grow FUBU. The lesson from John is that it does not matter what other people are doing; what matters is what you are doing with your time. Take advantage of the resources available to you now, not the resources you wish you had, so you can increase your knowledge for your next move in life.

Study Hard and Get a Good Job Won't Cut It Anymore

For many of us the money advice we received growing up was get a good education, even if you go into significant student debt, and get a well-paying job to climb the corporate ladder. This advice implied you would probably work for one or two employers until you were age 65. The advice suggests a generous retirement package and a financially stress-free retirement.

Unfortunately, this advice, on its own, is insufficient for the modern economy. A 2017/2018 Global Benefits Attitudes Survey of workers found that more than a third of those surveyed expect to retire after age 70 due to financial reasons, usually a lack of savings. In addition, the Bureau of Consumer Financial Protection reports that a quarter of adults 62 and older are financially insecure. Looking at the current financial situation, the study hard/get a good job advice has clearly not worked for most people.

Where Did My Benefits Go?

The generous pensions and lifetime health care offered by most employers have all but disappeared. Today less than 16% of workers are provided defined benefit pensions that were once commonplace. Many companies have also switched to using contractors or part-time workers to reduce labor costs. Since the early 1970s average wages have stagnated, rising barely .02% per year in inflation adjusted dollars. As jobs now tend to have fewer retirement and health insurance benefits, it shifts a greater financial burden on employees. This is why it is so incumbent on you to act now and take charge of your long-term financial plans.

The traditional study hard/get a good job advice also neglects the fact that the cost of a college education or a graduate degree has skyrocketed in the last two decades. It is true that those with a college degree earn significantly more during their working life. But many of these workers are trapped under massive student loans. Student loan debt can lock you into a career whether you like it or not. Also, college is not a viable option for everyone. According to census data in 2017 only 33.4% of workers over the age of 25 have a college degree. This means most workers don't have a college degree, but they still need a path to financial freedom.

New Advice: Build Multiple Revenue Streams

The study hard/get a good job advice overlooks the real key to wealth creation, which is generating multiple revenue streams that buys your financial freedom. It also overlooks the importance of tracking where your money goes to ensure that your expenditures are reasonable and meaningful. Following the traditional advice puts off retirement for so long that you miss out on many years where you could be pursuing other interests, expanding your skills, and spending quality time with friends and family. The rules of the game have changed and a new approach is required.

Don't Be a Chump, Loyalty is a Two-Way Street

Employers still expect workers to commit to the job, but unfortunately most no longer provide the benefits they once did. That is why choosing where to work is such an important decision. In addition to adequate benefits, a good employer should provide opportunities to help you develop your skills to excel. Your goal is to grow and learn while helping the company become more profitable.

But *loyalty is a two-way street.* If your employer does not offer such opportunities and your skills are stagnating, you need to be more judicious with your loyalty. Don't be a chump sitting in a job that will never get you where you hope to go. Spend the time to research better employment options, don't stay with an employer thinking it will get better, because it probably won't. Remember it is your responsibility to make your luck and every move you make between employers should advance your financial freedom goals. Fortunately, as you follow the plan you create from reading this book and the corresponding *10 Stages Workbook* you will reduce your expenses and create multiple income streams, which will make you less beholden to an employer.

Life is a Race so Start Immediately

People frequently say that life is not a race. They are wrong; life is absolutely a race. *But it is not a competition. You are only racing against yourself and the prize is time.* Why take 45 years to achieve the goal of financial freedom when you could reach it in 20 years or less. Would you rather be financially free at 70 years old or 45 years old? Some minor modifications to your daily habits, spending, and creating side income can cut twenty to thirty years from your retirement timeline.

One of the reasons people don't view life as a race is because they have a hard time visualizing their future selves. Studies show that a person is more willing to save for retirement if they see an age progression photo of themselves. If you retain a mental image of what your future life will look like once you reach financial freedom, it will fuel your daily desire to make it reality.

Define Why You Want to Be Financially Free

It is important to take time away from life's distractions to think about why you want financial freedom. What do you want for your future self? Would you prefer to spend your time pursuing your musical talents, or becoming a pilot, or working at a meaningful charity? Do you just want more time to spend with family and friends? It may be a specific experience like having the time to write a novel, or ride a motorcycle through South America, or learning to cook in Italy. Whatever will motivate you, begin to write these things down. These specific goals help you stay committed to your plan. Delayed gratification is an important component of your long-term success and is a topic we will revisit.

Keep a List of Events, Places and Skills for Motivation

Personally, we maintain a list of events and places we hope to experience and skills we hope to learn. Each year we add a few more items to the list and check off the ones we have completed. This list is a regular reminder that adhering to our plan was well worth the time and effort.

Think about five things in the next few years that you always wanted to do. Maybe it is to go to the Super Bowl or spend a week at Disney World, or visit Paris or drive old Route 66 with some friends. It could be as simple as seeing a certain band in concert or visiting a specific museum or national park. Perhaps you want to learn how to weld, or code or surf. As you think about these events, places or skills, return to your *10 Stages Workbook* to write them down. These are five things you will achieve through your plan; check them off as you complete them and add a new one to the list.

Keep Your Eye on the Prize

Never lose sight of the fact that once your earnings from your multiple income streams equals your monthly expenses, full-time paid employment becomes optional. *Let that sink in a bit because it is a powerful thought. Your day job becomes optional.*

Everyday becomes a Saturday and you can chase the day wherever it takes you. You can simply spend the day volunteering, teaching, or pursuing your favorite sport or hobby. The choice becomes yours. The goal of financial freedom should always be forefront in your mind. During the day when you encounter new opportunities or if you are deciding whether to spend money, ask yourself if the expenditure is delaying or advancing your goal of financial freedom. This quickly becomes second nature and allows you to say no to counterproductive choices.

Financial Freedom as Financial Body Armor

As you think about motivations, also consider that financial freedom is like financial body armor. Most of us have had the unpleasant experience of working for a bad boss at some point in our career. I am pretty much convinced I once worked for a robot wearing human skin that was desperately trying to pass the Alan Turing test. Such an odd character. Bad bosses may be the micromanager or the credit stealer. But they also include the more serious cases of the bully, the screamer, and the sexual harasser.

Senior management may try to prevent such behavior, but these bad bosses still exist in every organization. Although I have worked for some truly inspiring and wonderful bosses, I have also had a few of these bad ones as well.

I encountered one soon after we reached financial independence. Colleagues warned me that our new boss regularly screamed at the staff. Upon hearing this I did not feel any sense of unease that would usually accompany such news. Why? Because it did not matter. I realized right then that financial freedom was financial body armor against these bosses. There was no way I was going to let this person scream at me.

Knowing you don't have to tolerate inappropriate or unprofessional behavior is remarkably empowering. Personally, this form of body armor has surprised me as one of the aspects of financial freedom I appreciate most. You can stand up for yourself without fear of the consequences. Perhaps this confidence was reflected in my general attitude, because in all my interactions with this boss over a year, I was never a recipient of the screaming. But I definitely knew I would not stand for it had it occurred.

Key Takeaways:

• You need to be creative in your planning; the traditional advice of study hard, go to college, and get a well-paying job does not work like it once did. The cost of an education has skyrocketed and many employers have cut once generous benefits. The nature of employment and benefits have become less secure and require more proactive efforts on your part as you navigate your career and build skills.

• You must be intellectually curious and take advantage of the resources available to you at your current stage in life to improve your situation. Make your luck. Don't wait until the timing or circumstances are better; you could be waiting forever.

• There are opportunities around you to make money and learn; seek them out, because fortune favors those who pay attention and are decisive.

• Define what will motivate you to stick to your plan and keep a list of places, events, and experiences you want to enjoy. The list will help keep you focused and on track.

• You do not want to be sitting in a job you don't enjoy for the next 20 years or at the mercy of a bad boss. Financial freedom is financial body armor, you won't have to put up with bad bosses or bad employers.

CHAPTER 4: FINANCIAL TERMS AND CONCEPTS

Before delving into the remaining chapters, it would be beneficial to review a few key terms and concepts everyone should know. If you already have a high level of financial literacy and these terms and concepts are a review, feel free to skim through. If not, please take the time to understand them before proceeding to the remaining sections because we will refer back to them regularly.

Key Terms and Concepts

Financial Independence, Retire Early (FIRE): There is a range of perspectives on what constitutes financial independence and retiring early. You can think about this as three levels:

• **Basic level:** This is where your income streams outside of a regular job cover your basic expenses such as housing, utilities, health care, food, and transportation.

• **Medium level:** At this level your outside income streams have fully replaced your job income. This allows you to quit your job while still maintaining the same lifestyle.

• **High level:** Here your income streams allow you to maintain your current lifestyle and provide additional income to invest and create new income streams.

Similarly, there are different views regarding the notion of retiring early. It could mean retiring at age 60 or 40. It is up to you to decide when to retire. For our purposes, retiring early does not mean you never work again; *it means you don't have to work again.* You may choose to augment your income through full-time or part-time employment after gaining financial independence. Temporary employment can be a great way to bring in additional money during market downturns for buying assets at a discount. Work may also be a way to keep an active network of contacts. *But a well-executed financial freedom plan ensures that work is optional and not mandatory.*

Net Worth: Net worth is calculated by taking all your assets (what you own) and subtracting all your liabilities (what you owe). For our purposes of net worth do not include personal property such as furniture, jewelry, electronics or anything you bought from the Franklin Mint among your assets. In the following chapters you will see why. If you owe more money than your assets are worth, you have a negative net worth. Reading this book will help change that. Regularly tracking your net worth is a way to measure your progress and to see which investments are increasing your wealth.

The 4% Rule and the Sustainable Withdrawal Rate: The 4% rule posits that you can safely withdraw 4% of your retirement portfolio each year and will have a 95% chance of not running out of money after 33 years. The rule says your portfolio must consist of 60% stocks and 40% bonds. The rule also allows you to increase the amount of your withdrawals by 2%-3% each year to keep up with inflation. For example, if you have a $1 million portfolio with a 60/40 mix of stocks and bonds you could withdraw $40,000 in your first year of retirement and $40,800 in the second year of retirement with the $800 being equal to the 2% increase for inflation.

The 4% rule assumes you will be consistent in your withdrawals and not splurge one year and withdraw less the next year. It also assumes you will not panic and sell your portfolio during down markets. The 4% rule is prospective, and it is back tested through history, but given the uncertainty of future events there is a risk that it may not work as well in the future. The 4% rule is attributed to both a 1994 article by William Bengen and a 1998 study by Trinity University in Texas. Bengen used stocks combined with intermediate-term government bonds and Trinity used stocks and corporate bonds in their portfolio but they arrived at the same conclusion.

The 4% rule is essentially the same as another common retirement strategy called the 25 times annual retirement income rule. For example, if you think you need $25,000 a year in retirement income you should accumulate a nest egg of $625,000 which is equal to $25,000 multiplied by 25. The 4% rule and the 25 times retirement income rule are not guaranteed, but they are a helpful guide for what investments you should have in your portfolio and how much you can expect to withdraw each year.

If you are planning for a retirement that lasts 40 or 50 years, consider using a more conservative withdraw rate of 3.5% or 3% per year instead of 4%. Similarly, if you use the 25 times retirement income approach you may want to save 28 or 30 times the annual retirement income you need to protect yourself from running out of money early. These more conservative strategies will prolong the number of years your portfolio can provide the expected annual income.

One caveat for these two rules is that if there is a major decline in stock prices in the first five years after you retire you should suspend your withdrawals and find alternative income sources like a part-time job. If you stop taking withdrawals it will allow your portfolio time to recover. If the stock market declines significantly in the first five years and you continue to take annual withdrawals, you may exhaust your portfolio in just 15 or 20 years.

Lifestyle Inflation: Lifestyle inflation refers to increasing your spending habits to match your rising income levels. It includes buying bigger homes, nicer clothes, fancier vehicles, and more luxury goods each time you get a raise. Lifestyle inflation is the antithesis of the plan in this book. A single splurge is fine, but increasing your spending for housing, transportation, food, and entertainment will make you more dependent on your job and deprive you of financial freedom.

Delayed Gratification: Delayed gratification is probably the single most important behavioral trait for achieving financial independence and creating wealth. It is the ability to resist accepting a smaller reward today, to obtain a far greater reward in the future. Put simply, I would rather not pay $100,000 today for a Tesla, when I can invest those funds for 20 years to create a revenue stream that could buy me a Tesla *every year*. Delayed gratification comes naturally to some people, while others must train themselves to patiently wait for future rewards. Accepting delayed gratification is a key part of strengthening your money mindset.

Cash Flow: Cash flow is the amount of cash and cash-equivalents being generated by a business or an investment. For example, the monthly cash flow on a rental property might be $300 per month or $3,600 per year. Your goal of creating multiple incomes streams is to generate various forms of cash flow.

Unsecured Debt: Unsecured debt is a debt obligation that is not supported by an underlying asset like real estate or collateral. Credit card debt is a common form of unsecured debt. It is important to note that the University of Michigan Health and Retirement Study on middle aged and older people has found that an individual's level of unsecured consumer debt will have a negative impact on their mental wellbeing. A higher amount of unsecured debt is also a significant predictor of symptoms of depression.

Debt Leverage: Debt is used as leverage to allow investors to control an asset by only putting down a fraction of the total price. For example, if you purchase a $100,000 house, you could use a down payment of $10,000 and finance the remaining $90,000 with a loan. You will pay off the loan in monthly payments over 15 to 30 years. Each payment consists of some principal and some interest. The interest is the cost of borrowing the money and the principal pays down the balance of the loan. The interest part of the payment declines over time as more of each successive payment consists of principal.

Investors use debt as leverage because it can dramatically increase their annual returns. For example, if you buy $10,000 worth of stock in a company and a year later the stock increases in value by 10% you have made a return of $1,000. $10,000 x 10% = $1,000. However, if you use $10,000 as a down payment to buy a $100,000 house (financing the other $90,000) and a year later the house goes up in value by 10% to $110,000, the return on your $10,000 is 100%. You invested $10,000 and the house went up in value by $10,000, so you were able to double your money by using leverage.

Just as leverage can dramatically increase your returns it can also dramatically increase your losses. If the same house declined in value from $100,000 to $90,000 then your $10,000 would have gone to zero after a year. *Remember when it comes to investing you lock in your gains or losses when you sell.* If the house falls in value to $90,000 but you held it, the house may soon increase again in value to $100,000 and you won't lose any money because you didn't sell.

Being able to hold on to your assets when they decline in value is a way to protect yourself from having to realize these losses. From 2006 to 2009 the decline in real estate prices wiped out $6 trillion in household wealth. People who lost this wealth did so because they had to sell their assets when prices were low. Holding some cash reserves protects you from having to sell assets in these downturns and can help you buy assets at a discount. We will discuss this topic in more detail in future chapters.

Debt Ratio: Debt ratio is a financial tool to measure the extent of debt being used by an individual or a business. The ratio is the total debt divided by the total assets and the answer is shown as a decimal or percentage. For example, if a person's only debt is a $100,000 mortgage and they have assets including the home, worth $300,000, their debt ratio would be 100,000/300,000 = .33 or 33%.

The debt ratio is a measurement that lenders use to assess the ability of a borrower to repay a loan. A higher debt ratio indicates a person or business is highly leveraged with debt and may have trouble repaying the debt because they don't have other assets generating income or assets they can sell to help cover the loan payments.

Investing in stocks and bonds allows you to build a portfolio of assets that will lower your overall debt ratio. The lender views these assets as reserves that can be sold to pay off debt. Thus, these assets increase your ability to qualify for loans which in turn can be used as leverage to purchase additional income producing assets. For example, if you have $25,000 in a portfolio of stocks and you apply for a mortgage to buy a $200,000 house this stock portfolio will help you qualify for the loan.

Return on Investment (ROI): Return on investment is a measurement to evaluate the efficiency of an investment. It also allows you to compare different investments to see which might provide you the highest return on your money. To find the ROI, divide the expected return of the investment by the cost of the investment. If I anticipate a return of $8,000 after one year on a $50,000 investment, my expected ROI is 16% ($8,000/$50,000 = 0.16 or 16%).

If the expected return is $8,000 after *two years* instead of just one, the ROI would be 8% per year because the return of 16% is divided by 2 years instead of one (0.16/2 =0.08). An important lesson to remember is ROI is the *expected return*, many things could happen with the investment that could result in a return that is either higher or lower than the expected ROI.

<u>Asset Bubbles and Crashes:</u> Periodically assets will go into bubble territory where investors have irrational expectations of their future returns, thus leading people to significantly overpay for these assets. The bubble is usually followed by a crash in prices. It happened with technology stocks in 1999 and real estate in 2007-2008. It even occurs with items that are not usually viewed as assets including tulip bulbs in the Netherlands in 1636-1637 and the plush toys Beanie Babies in the mid-1990s. Needless to say, once the popularity wanes, people lose significant amounts of money.

<u>Inflation's Impact on Purchasing Power</u>: The prices of goods and services tend to rise over time, usually due to inflation which may be 2% to 3% per year. An apple that costs $1 today may cost $1.03 next year. Inflation reduces the purchasing power of money over time because you need more dollars to purchase the same amount of goods. There are certainly exceptions to this rule; consumer electronics tend to decline in price over time due to advances in technology and manufacturing which make them cheaper to produce. That is why a flat screen television that once cost $1,500 will cost $500 a few years later. Also, inflation depends on where you live; some countries regularly have double digit annual inflation rates.

<u>Inflation Example: $1 Million in 1987 vs 2017</u>: My favorite way to demonstrate inflation is to look at the decreasing purchasing power of $1 million over 30 years. If you were handed $1 million in 1987 you could buy an average priced home for $127,200 and a new Toyota Corolla for approximately $9,348. The remaining $863,452 was equal to 53 times the 1987 average per capita income of $16,265. This amount would be more than enough money to retire if you used the 25 times income rule that we discussed earlier. It would be 53 times the average income in the country at the time.

However, if you were handed that same $1 million in 2017 your purchase of an average priced home would be $369,900, the new Toyota Corolla would cost about $21,585 and the remaining $608,515 is equal to just 12 times the average per capita income of $50,392. *This illustrates the importance of factoring in the effect of inflation over time and how it will decrease the purchasing power of your income in the future.* Just remember $1 today is worth far more than $1 in 30 years.

Downside Risk: Downside risk is a way of factoring in the potential for things to go wrong. Choosing to wear a suit instead of a clown suit to a job interview is a way to reduce your downside risk. Investors use downside risk to estimate the decline in value of an investment if market conditions change. Downside risk can be used either to explain a worst-case scenario for an investment or estimate how much you may lose in response to certain events.

When building a long-term plan for financial independence you must incorporate downside risk assumptions to protect yourself, because some things will go wrong. There will be times when the stock market plummets, businesses fail, real estate values decline, rental properties face extended vacancies, taxes increase, health care costs rise, or government benefits are reduced. Include these types of downside risk assumptions in your plan.

Capital Gain: The profit made from selling an investment, property or other asset. If you lost money from the sale it is a capital loss.

The Power of Compounding Interest: Albert Einstein is quoted as saying, "the power of compound interest is the most powerful force in the universe." Think of compounding interest as the turbocharger powering the growth in your savings. For example, Vanessa is 20 years old and she invests $5,000 earning a 7% return per year. Vanessa never adds another dollar, but she allows the money and the interest to be reinvested every year. At age 50 Vanessa will have $38,061. At age 60 Vanessa will have

$74,872 and at age 70 she will have $147,285. Not bad Vanessa!

The next example shows how just a 1.5% higher annual return, compounded over time, will dramatically increase Vanessa's wealth. This 1.5% increase will add nearly $150,000 over a fifty-year period on Vanessa's investment of $5,000. Bravo Vanessa, Bravo!

Age 50	7% = $38,061	8.5% = $57,791
Age 60	7% = $74,871	8.5% = $130,665
Age 70	7% = $147,285	8.5% = $295,430

Closely review every fee on the investments in your portfolio, because getting a slightly higher return or eliminating a fee of ½% or 1% per year can change your lifetime return by hundreds of thousands of dollars.

Key Takeaways:

•   You don't need to be particularly skilled in math or finance to become wealthy, but you do need to understand the basic calculations and strategies explained in this chapter. This includes the 4% withdrawal rate and its twin the 25 times income rule. Also understand that a major market correction in the first five years of retirement means you will have to return to working and suspend your withdrawals until your assets recover.

•   You need to determine your appetite for risk and what financial independence and retiring early mean to you. Determine if retirement means working part-time with a moderate portfolio or waiting until you have a larger portfolio that covers all your expenses with additional income left over to invest.

•   Be able to calculate your debt ratio and recognize the importance of using debt wisely to purchase income producing assets. Review the fees and rates of return on your investments because 1% per year can mean the difference of $100,000 or more over your lifetime.

• Realize that inflation will reduce the future purchasing power of your money as we saw with the example of $1 million in 1987 versus $1 million in 2017.

• You must conduct due diligence and run the numbers on any investment. Also understand what assumptions you are making regarding the potential performance of that investment. Be cautious of irrational exuberance; the hysteria that forms during asset bubbles can lead to tragic decisions and major losses.

• Among your downside risk considerations think about corrections in the stock market or real estate sector, the potential for your businesses to fail, rental property vacancies, increased future tax rates and health care costs. Not all these events will happen at the same time, but your portfolio needs to be able to withstand these types of risks.

CHAPTER 5: TYPES OF INCOME AND TAXES

If someone offers you $100 in wages or $100 in investment income do you know which one puts more money in your pocket after taxes? Not all income is taxed the same. Wage income from a traditional job incurs the highest tax rates, which is unfortunate for most people because it is the majority of their income. In this chapter we will explore different types of income and how they are taxed. Bear with me as these concepts are a bit dry. I have added examples to help illustrate the lessons. These concepts can't be overlooked; they were a crucial part of our plan. Taking the time to understand them is important for your long-term success.

As you read this chapter, recognize that tax rates and tax rules change from year to year and from one country to the next. This chapter is designed to teach you that there are certain types of income and each type is taxed differently. You will have to expand on this information by doing some research on taxes in the country and state where you live. For more details on U.S. taxes see the section on taxes on the Loaded for Life website.

Three Types of Income and Losses

As you create your plan expect to have three different types of income:

1) Active income;

2) Portfolio income; and

3) Passive income.

As mentioned above, these distinct types of income are taxed differently. Also, losses you incur in one category may only be applied to income in that same category, with a few exceptions that we will dis-

cuss below.

1) **Active Income:** Think of active income (or losses) as the income you earn from taking action or performing a service. It is when you commit your time to do a job and are paid for it. Active income includes income from salaries, tips, commissions, or self-employment income from running a business. Active income is what most employees are paid.

In situations where you are running a business, there is generally a requirement that you *materially participated* or actively managed the business for the income to be deemed active income. This is the difference between a person who works in the business and a silent partner who invests in the business, but doesn't work in the business.

2) **Portfolio Income:** Portfolio income (or losses) is when you are not directly performing a service to create the income. Portfolio income is earned when an investment or a thing you created is generating income. For example, interest on a savings accounts or from a bond you own is portfolio income. If you earn royalties from creative works such as books or songs you wrote or photographs you took it is portfolio income. **Capital gains from selling appreciated assets are also portfolio income, as are dividends you receive from stocks you own.**

For example, let's say you buy $10,000 of Microsoft stock and sell it for $11,000 two years later. While you owned the stock, Microsoft paid you $200 in dividends. You have a capital gain of $1,000 from the stock appreciating in value and $200 in dividends, both of these are portfolio income. **This is also a great example of how you can earn multiple income streams from an investment.**

3) **Passive Income:** Passive income (or losses) is usually from a business in which you *do not materially participate, sort of the opposite of active income.* If you invested $25,000 in your cousin

Vinny's restaurant in return for a percentage of the profits, but have no other involvement with Vinny's business, your earnings would most likely be passive income. Passive losses cannot be used to offset gains from active income or portfolio income unless certain factors apply. Usually you need other passive income to offset your passive losses.

There are also situations where the government will limit the amount of passive losses you can take per tax year. If so, you will need to carry the losses forward to the next tax year to offset future passive income. For example, your $25,000 Vinny's restaurant investment led to a passive loss of $2,000 the first year. Vinny was just starting up and still trying to attract customers. You can carry this loss forward if you have no other passive income for the year.

In the following year Vinny wins the award for best cheesesteak in the city and he becomes more profitable. You earn $3,000 in passive income from the restaurant for the year. You would only pay tax on $1,000 of this passive income because the previous $2,000 loss would offset the other $2,000 in passive income. See below:

Vinny's Restaurant Investment: $25,000
Year 1: Passive Loss: -$2,000
Year 2: Passive Income: $3,000
Year 2: Taxable income: $1,000 ($3,000 - $2,000 loss)

Please note: passive losses related to real estate activity requires a more detailed explanation that is available on the Loaded for Life website.

Taking Losses from One Category of Income to Another

Since all of us periodically make bad investments there is an exception which allows you to take up to $3,000 in capital losses each year against your active income. For example, if you bought Microsoft stock for $10,000 but sold it for $7,000, your $3,000 loss can be deducted against the active income from your job. Hence, you will pay a little less in income tax this year because of this loss.

Losses above $3,000 can be used to offset other capital gains or carried forward to the next tax year to be deducted. For example, if your loss on Microsoft stock was $4,000, you could take $3,000 against active income from your job this year and then take the remaining $1,000 loss against your job income next year. It is a little way to help soften the financial blow of these losses.

Bought Microsoft Stock: $7,000
Sold Microsoft Stock: $3,000 ($4,000 loss)
Passive Loss Year 1: -$3,000 (against active income)
Passive Loss Year 2: -$1,000 (against active income)

If you find you have significant tax losses year after year, your problem is not taxes, it is your stock picking strategy. The best approach for stock investing is usually to buy a broad index of stocks which we will discuss more in future chapters.

Income, Social Security and Medicare Taxes

Your country may also tax income to help pay for pensions for older retirees as a form of social security. For example, in the United States in 2019, active income up to $132,900 is subject to the Federal Insurance Contributions Act (FICA) tax of 7.65% which covers Social Security Retirement Benefits and Medicare (health care services). This FICA tax does not apply to passive income and portfolio income, which means you save 7.65% in taxes on that type of income. In addition, an equal amount of this 7.65% FICA tax is also paid by your employer to help support these government programs.

Therefore, if you have $50,000 in active income you and your employer will each pay $3,825 in FICA taxes. However, if you have $50,000 in portfolio or passive income you will not pay any FICA taxes. This is one of the reasons investors want to create passive and portfolio income, as it allows them to pay less in taxes and keep more of what they earn.

Review your country's respective tax rates to identify how much of your income is taxed to pay for public pensions or public healthcare for retirees. Also check to see if active income is taxed differently than passive income or portfolio income.

Marginal Tax Rates

Most countries, including the United States, use marginal tax rates on income at the federal level. Accordingly, it helps to understand how marginal tax rates work. When filing your personal federal income tax return, you fall into one of four categories. This is referred to as your filing status and the four categories are below.

Tax Filing Status:

<u>Single</u>: A single person;
<u>Married Filing Jointly</u>: A couple with or without children;
<u>Married Filing Separate</u>: A couple filing separate tax returns; this filing status has several disadvantages compared to filing jointly and is therefore not covered in as much detail;
<u>Head of Household</u>: A single person with an additional person in the household who is a dependent.

Each category of tax filer is eligible for a standard deduction or exemption, which allows filers to subtract some of their income before any income tax is applied. The reason for this is part of a taxpayer's income must be used for purchasing essentials (food and shelter) which the government does not seek to tax. It helps people with lower incomes keep more of what they earn. Note that the standard deduction amount can change from year to year. The 2019 figures are below:

<u>Example Standard Deduction Based on Filing Status:</u>
Single $12,200
Married Filing Jointly $24,400
Married Filing Separately $12,200
Head of Household $18,350

Note: The United States allow filers to compile eligible tax deductions expenses in an itemized list. This approach is referred to as itemizing. Itemized deductions may include mortgage interest and property taxes on a primary residence (up to a limit) or business expenses that are not reimbursed by your employer. The details of itemizing are well beyond the scope of this chapter, but is something for you to investigate further if it would be advantageous for you to itemize.

How Marginal Tax Rates Work

With marginal tax rates, your income is separated into brackets and taxed at increasingly higher rates for each bracket. It makes people with higher incomes pay more tax. It may be easier to think of these tax brackets as a bucket you fill. Once you have filled the bucket of a tax bracket to the maximum amount allowed, you move on to the next bucket. An example of marginal tax rates for each tax filing category are below. *These are the tax rates that apply to income above the standard deduction. If you make less than the standard deduction you pay $0 in federal income tax.*

Marginal Tax Rate	Single	Married Filing Joint	Married Filing Separate	Head of Household
10%	$0-$9,700	$0 to $19,400	$0 to $9,700	$0 to $13,850
12%	$9,701-$39,475	$19,401 to $78,950	$9,701 to $39,475	$13,851 to $52,850
22%	$39,476 - $84,200	$78,951 to $168,400	$39,476 to $84,200	$52,851 to $84,200
24%	$84,201 - $160,725	$168,401 to $321,450	$84,201 to $160,725	$84,201 to $160,700
32%	$160,725 - $204,100	$321,451 to $408,200	$160,726 to $204,100	$160,701 to $204,100
35%	$204,101 - $510,300	$408,201 to $612,350	$204,101 to $306,175	$204,101 to $510,300
37%	$510,301 or more	$612,351 or more	$306,176 or more	$510,301 or more

Effective Tax Rate versus Marginal Tax Rate

Look at the chart above and assume you are single and earn a salary of $52,200. We would subtract the first $12,200 in income as your standard deduction leaving you with $40,000 in taxable income. The chart above shows your income is within the 22% marginal tax bracket, so the next dollar of income you earn is taxed at 22%. However, and this is important, not all your income is taxed at 22% rate. Most of your income was taxed at 12% and the first $9,700 in income was taxed at 10%. The tax rate you pay is called your *effective tax rate and it will be lower than your marginal rate.*

You would be surprised how often people get this wrong. I have had many people tell me they are in the 24% tax bracket and mistakenly believe all their income is being taxed at 24%. It is only that next dollar of income earned that is taxed at the 24% rate. Once you hit the ceiling of the 24% tax bracket your marginal tax rate jumps to 32%

Marginal Income Tax Example:

This example will tie everything together, so just stay with me for a few more minutes. Alex is single, and her only source of income is her job. She earned $52,200 for the year. Her federal income tax would be broken down like this:

Alex's income	$52,200
Standard deduction	-$12,200
Taxable income	$40,000

- Alex's first $9,700 of income is taxed at 10% which equals $970 in tax.
- Next, her income from $9,701 to $39,475 falls within the 12% tax bracket, which equals $3,573 in tax.
- Finally, her income from $39,476 to $40,000 falls in the 22% tax bracket, which for Alex equals $116 in tax.
- If we add these taxes together Alex's total income tax is $4,659.

Alex is in the 22% marginal tax bracket, but her total federal income taxes were only $4,659 on taxable income of $40,000. Alex's *effective tax rate* is 11.6% because part of her income fell within the 10% bracket and most of her income was in the 12% bracket. Only her last $524 in earnings is taxed at a rate of 22%.

Knowing how tax brackets work helps you see how much tax applies to the next dollar you earn. Note that this example only includes Alex's marginal income tax, it does not include other taxes like FICA which we discussed previously.

Flat Tax Rates

If a country or state does not use a marginal tax rate, it will likely use a flat tax rate. We see this in some of the Baltic states in Europe or individual states within the United States. With a flat tax the government has a set tax rate such as 20% that applies to all income above a certain level. We can use Alex again as an example to explain how a flat tax works.

Flat Income Tax Example

Alex earned $52,200 for the year and her country has an exemption for the first $15,000 of income. Her federal income tax would be broken down like this:

> Alex's income $52,200
>
> Exemption   -$15,000
>
> Taxable income $37,000

We multiply Alex's taxable income by the flat tax rate of 20% ($37,000 x .20 = $7,400) which means Alex will pay $7,400 in income tax.

Capital Gains and Taxes

We are going to return to the topic of capital gains which we discussed under portfolio income to further explain some tax implications. We already said that you can take up to $3,000 per year in capital losses against your active income, such as income from your job. U.S. federal government also taxes capital gains based on how long you held the asset, for example:

Short-term capital gains: Taxed at a higher rate for assets held for a year or less.

Long-term capital gains: Taxed at a lower rate for assets held for more than a year and a day. Think of it as the government trying to give you an incentive to hold assets or investments for a longer period.

In addition, capital gains tax rates are often *lower* than the regular marginal income tax rates, which means your portfolio income from investments is taxed at a lower rate than the active income from your job.

Below is an example of capital gains rates based on different tax filing status. As you look at the example below, note that in 2019 if you are married and filing a joint tax return and your income is below $78,750 you will not pay any tax on capital gains. If you have some investments that have gone up in value you could sell them and lock in those gains while paying no federal income tax. The same rule applies if you are single and earn less than $39,375. This is what I mean by learning how the tax code works so you can use it to your advantage. This strategy is a great way to earn tax-free profits every year. Just a little research can show you ways to save hundreds or thousands of dollars on your taxes.

Capital Gains Tax Rates

Tax rate	Filing Single	Married Filing Joint	Filing as Head of Household
0%	$0-$39,375	$0-$78,750	$0-$52,750
15% tax bracket	$39,376 to $434,550	$78,751 to $488,850	$52,751 to $461,700
20% tax bracket	$434,551 or more	$488,851 or more	$461,701 or more

State and Local Income Taxes

Similar to federal taxes you may also pay taxes at the state or local level. These taxes can be a marginal tax or flat tax. These state and local taxes may apply to active income, passive income and portfolio income or all three categories depending on your location. Fortunately, you usually get a tax deduction for the income you used to pay federal taxes. For example, U.S. states usually only tax the income leftover after you pay your Federal income tax.

Where you live can make a huge difference in the amount of tax you pay. A neighboring state may have much lower tax rates, or they may exempt certain types of income from taxes. For example, in the United States at the time of writing there were seven states that do not have personal income tax: Alaska, Florida, Nevada, South Dakota, Texas, Washington and Wyoming. This means if you live in Illinois you pay a State income tax rate of 4.95% but if you live in Florida you pay $0. *Where you choose to live has a tremendous impact on your after-tax income.* The less you pay in taxes the more you have to invest in your plan for financial freedom.

Learning More About Taxes

Okay, that is it. We are now done with taxes, thanks for your patience. However, you still have work to do, and there are many ways to increase your knowledge about taxes. Start with some basic books on taxes and read the websites and publications available from your country's tax authority, such as the Internal Revenue Service. There are also posts on taxes on www.loadedforlife.com.

As a second step, try to get some firsthand practical experience in completing taxes. In the United States you can volunteer for the Internal Revenue Service's Volunteer Income Tax Assistance (VITA) program. The IRS will teach you about taxes, so you can volunteer to provide free tax preparation services to lower income earners. I have done it and the training and experience is excellent. A second option is to work part-time during the tax season with one of the major tax preparers like H&R Block or Liberty Tax. Don't underestimate the importance of knowing about income types and how it is taxed. It is crucial for your future financial success.

Key Takeaways:

• Taxes are a vital component of your long-term planning, so you must have a basic understanding of how taxes work and how to take advantage of various tax strategies.

• You want to understand how marginal tax and flat tax rates apply to income. You also want to recognize how a standard deduction or similar exemption can shield some of your income from taxes.

• You should know the difference between active income, portfolio income and passive income. Losses from one category of income usually cannot offset income from another category, except in certain cases, such as when capital losses of up to $3,000 per year can be used to offset active income from your job.

• Understand the difference between marginal tax rates and effective tax rates. Tax rates and deductions change from year to year, but if you understand how taxes work it is relatively easy to keep up with these annual changes.

• Obtain practical experience in completing taxes as a volunteer with VITA or the equivalent in your country or consider working part-time for a professional tax preparer.

CHAPTER 6: WEALTH AND HOURLY RATES

How much money do you need to be comfortable for the rest of your life? Or to be wealthy? The average American believes it takes $1.4 million to be financially comfortable and $2.3 million to be wealthy. Your number may be higher or lower depending on your lifestyle. One of the goals of this book is to help you identify the amount you need in annual income to be financially free. To find this number you need to think beyond just a dollar amount for your basic living expenses and identify your other life goals. You need to think about future expenses for travel, educating kids, caring for elderly parents, and health care.

Think about what you spend money on each day that adds real value to your life and determine what you can cut as you work towards financial independence. You want to be enjoying life while you are preparing for your future. The goal of this book is not to get you to work as much as possible, saving everything you earn, for some great future reward. You need to have some fun along the way and if you enjoy the journey you will be more inclined to stick with your plan.

But you will need to start writing all of this down, either on paper or electronically. It is worth knowing that only one in four people have a written financial plan but the Schwab Modern Wealth Index shows having a written plan is proven to develop better daily money habits including regular saving and effectively managing debt. It is also worth noting that 92% of successful millionaires developed a long-term plan for their money. That is why this book has a corresponding *10 Stages Workbook*, I know how important having a written step-by-step action plan was for us in achieving our goals. This formula should work for you, the same way it did for us, but you have to follow all the steps and you can't cut corners.

Focus on the Cash Flow, Not Portfolio Size

One of the first steps to finding your financial freedom numbers is to realize that the actual dollar amount of your nest egg is not nearly as important as the amount of cash flow being generated by your investments. A million-dollar portfolio in a savings account with a paltry 1% annual return will only provide $10,000 in annual income. But five rental properties worth $500,000 might generate cash flow of $500 per property which is $30,000 in annual income. *Where your money is invested is more important than how much is invested.* This is a subject that we will discuss in far more detail throughout the book.

More Does Not Always Mean Better

An interesting fact about income levels is that happiness increases as a person's income increases but only until a certain peak is reached; afterwards each additional dollar will have less of an impact on your happiness. This is what economists refer to as diminishing marginal utility. Psychologists from University of Virginia and Purdue University completed a study looking at World Gallup Poll data covering 164 countries and 1.7 million people to assess their satisfaction in life and their respective earnings. What they found was that individuals with an annual income equivalent to $60,000 to $75,000 reach a sense of happiness and emotional well-being. Upping this income level to $95,000 per year will allow some individuals to obtain a higher level of satisfaction, but additional income beyond this level does not promote more happiness *and in some people can reduce their levels of happiness.*

The reason is that as people reach these higher income levels, they are more prone to compare their wealth status to others or to pursue material possessions. As we discussed in chapter 2 money does not buy status and material possessions do not create true happiness. This is the classic mistake of trying to keep up with the Joneses, spending money to impress other people or create the impression that you are wealthier than your peers. *If you equate spending money with happiness, you are setting yourself up to be disappointed.*

Social Media Can Fuel Overspending

This issue is more acute with the prevalence of social media. Studies from Allianz Life and Fidelity investments show that the desire to project an image of wealth on social media is having a negative impact on spending habits and financial well-being, particularly among Millennials. These results may soon apply to Generation Z if the trend continues. If this is a trap that you fall into you need to be conscious of it and look for ways to avoid the social media triggers that make you want to spend. One way to help you avoid overspending is to get a clear understanding of how much you actually earn. As you will see in the example below, many people overestimate what they really earn.

Calculate Your Real Hourly Rate

Many people look at their total salary and give little thought to determining what they earn on a per hour basis. The results can be a bit of a shock. The idea of calculating my hourly rate first occurred to me when a friend said he had a job making $100,000 a year. I thought this was a very high salary until I learned he was working 80 hours a week. Really, he had two 40 hour a week jobs that each paid $50,000. And as we learned in chapter 5, his "second job" was being taxed at a higher marginal rate.

There are several methods for calculating your hourly rate, from the basic to the advanced. A simple formula for a person working 40 hours a week is to divide your annual salary by 2,080 hours. Using this formula, we see that a person with an annual salary of $40,000 is making $19.23 per hour

($40,000/2080).

<u>Quick Calculation Trick</u>: A simplified version of this formula is to take your salary on the left side of the comma and divide by two. A $40,000 salary becomes $40 and when you divide by two the hourly rate is $20, which is close to the $19.23 above.

<u>After Federal Tax Rate:</u> In chapter 5 we explained marginal and effective tax rates. For our $20 per hour example we will apply an *effective* tax rate of 15% which equals $3 in taxes ($20 x .15 = $3). If we subtract the $3 in taxes, we find our *after-tax* rate is $17 per hour ($20 - $3 = $17).

<u>After State and Local Tax Rate:</u> We also need to subtract state or local income tax from the $17. If our effective state income tax rate is 3%, we multiply $17 by 3% which equals $0.51. We subtract this $0.51 from $17 for a total of $16.49. The states with lower or no income tax start to look much more appealing when you see $0.51 in tax deducted every hour from your salary.

<u>Actual Hours Worked</u>: If you want to take this calculation one step further, add in the actual number of hours you work each week if it is consistently more than 40 hours *and you are not paid overtime*. If a person works an average of 4 hours more per week, they work 208 more hours per year, so our $40,000 salary is divided by 2,288 hours. See below how these extra four hours per week lower our hourly earnings.

Hourly Rates	*40 Hour Week*	*44 Hour Week*
Pre-Tax Rate	$20	$18.18
After 15% Federal Taxes	$17	$15.18
After 3% State Tax	$16.49	$14.67

<u>Note</u>: The extra hours per week do not change your tax rate because you are not being paid more for the additional time.

<u>Factor in Your Commute</u>: You can also factor in your commute to and from work to your hourly rate. The average U.S. com-

mute time is 25 minutes, so I prefer to calculate any time above the 25-minute average, since most workers expect to have some form of a commute for their job. If you commute 55-minutes each morning and evening, it adds an additional hour to your workday (30 minutes in the morning and 30 minutes at night).

If we factor in these five extra commuting hours each week, it adds 260 hours to the year for a total of 2,340 hours. See below how a long commute lowers our hourly rate.

Hourly Rates for	25-minute commute	55-minute commute
Pre-Tax Rate	$20	$17.77
After 15% Federal Taxes	$17	$14.77
After 3% State Tax	$16.49	$14.26

Note: The tax rate remains the same because the commuting time does not change your tax rate.

A long commute will reduce your hourly income and will add to your overall monthly expenses by also increasing your transportation expenses, such as longer distances on the train or the subway or more wear and tear and fuel for your vehicle. We will look at ways to reduce your transportation costs in the next chapter. If you are working 44 hours per week and have this extra hour of commuting each day, your hourly rate falls to $12.19. This is significantly lower than the $20 in *pretax* dollars we started with and why I said many people overestimate what they earn each year.

Accurate Data on Your Hourly Income

Using these methods provides you with an accurate accounting of what you earn per hour. You can use the data to consider other jobs that are closer to where you live or require fewer hours per week to see if they actually pay a higher per hour rate. In addition, a different career may be more interesting or provide a better work/life balance for the same per hour rate you currently earn. Later in the book we will discuss shifting your thinking away from trading time for money, but for now focus on applying these tools to get the best return on a per hour basis for your job.

Purchases in Terms of Time Instead of Dollars

You may have thought you made $25 per hour, but after taxes, a long commute and extra hours worked you now realize you only make $16 per hour. Once you know your real hourly rate you begin to see how much work is required for the things you purchase. For example, at a rate of $16 per hour a $4 coffee is 15 minutes of work; an $80 new shirt is five hours of work; a night out of drinks and dinner for $128 is 8 hours of work, and a car costing $32,000 is 2,000 hours of work. *Once you realize how many hours you must work to pay for these items you tend to be more judicious with your spending.*

A way to incorporate this into your daily life is to take just a few moments to let your rational brain think about the real costs of a purchase, in terms of hours worked, before you buy. I used this approach when I first returned from Africa and it became second nature. I thought more about each purchase to make sure I really wanted it. It quickly led to a significant decline in my daily spending.

Raise Your Income to Increase Your Hourly Rate

Before we move away from the topic of calculating hourly rates and discuss ways to lower expenses, I want to cover the topic of raising your income. One of the fastest ways to improve your hourly rate is through a raise or promotion. And sometimes it can be as simple as asking for one.

I mentioned in the introduction of this book that my first job had an annual salary of $24,000. I accepted the job from Morocco and was unaware of the cost of living in Washington D.C. I also did not really know what my skills were worth in the job market. I worked with a great group of people and I was committed to working hard. But after doing some research I thought I was being underpaid compared to people in a similar position and with similar skills. With this information in hand I asked my boss if we could schedule a meeting. In calm professional manner, I asked him what he thought was possible to get me closer to the market rate for my skills and experience. In a few days he offered me a raise of $10,000. Based on my research $34,000 was much closer to the market rate.

This was a very valuable lesson, *you can't receive what you don't ask for, so ask for what you want in life.* If I kept quiet, I would have missed this opportunity to dramatically increase my salary. In these situations, you really have nothing to lose. If my boss had said no, I would be in the same position I was already in. Before you ask for a raise, do your due diligence, have examples of what other people in your same position are making and be in a position where you have already proven your value to the company.

If your employer can't or won't increase your salary, then it may be time to look for a new job. Over time staying with the same employer tends to erode your earnings. Strategically making job changes is a way to increase your salary by between 10%-20% depending on your career field. Also factor in proximity to work and options for public transport that could further reduce transportation costs and commuting times to increase your hourly rate.

Key Takeaways:

• The average American believes it takes $1.4 million to be financially comfortable and $2.3 million to be wealthy. This is a starting point for you to determine what you think you will need for financial freedom.

• The size of your portfolio is not as important as the returns being generated by your portfolio; focus on a strong monthly cash flow and have a written plan. Those with a written plan are proven to be more successful.

• A sense of financial wellbeing can be achieved with $60,000 to $75,000 per year, but more than $95,000 per year may actual diminish your sense of financial wellbeing.

• Calculate your hourly wage by factoring the total numbers of hours you work, the cost of taxes, and extra time commuting. Knowing what you truly make per hour helps you more accurately compare other job opportunities that might be a better choice.

• Learn to calculate purchases based on your real hourly rate and take a few minutes before you make a purchase to ensure it is a wise decision.

• One of the best ways to increase your hourly rate is to obtain a raise and it can be as simple as just asking. Before you ask, prove you are an excellent employee and do your research to justify your request for a raise. You want to present the facts in a calm and persuasive manner. If your employer says no, it may be time to find a new employer.

CHAPTER 7: AVERAGE HOUSEHOLD EXPENSES

Average Household Spending

A good starting point for determining how much annual income you might need is to look at the average level of income and spending per U.S. household. *Remember this is per household not per person and similar data exists for other countries.* According to the latest data (2016) from the Consumer Expenditure Survey from the U.S. Bureau of Labor Statistics (BLS) the average yearly income of a household is $74,664 *before taxes*.

The BLS definition of income is relatively broad and includes traditional wage income, self-employment income, investment income (interest and dividends), retirement fund cash benefits, rental income, Social Security benefits, veteran's cash benefits, unemployment and worker's compensation, as well as public assistance cash payments.

Since some of this income will be used to pay taxes, we again use the BLS data to deduct for annual taxes (federal, state and local) which equal $10,489. This means the average household's *after-tax* income is **$64,175**.

Please note: The BLS data does not provide details on every type of expense, some expenses are lumped together. The data shows that $6,863 of annual spending is used for items such as gifts and paying consumer debt including credit card debt. If a household can reduce its credit card debt, more income can be used for other expenses or to invest. We will cover the negative impact of credit card debt in more detail later.

Top Five Categories of Expenses

Now let's look at how the average household spends this **$64,175** in after-tax income. The data shows five major expense categories which include:

1. **Housing** accounts for $18,886 or 29.4% of after-tax income. The category for housing includes owned and rented houses, utilities, furnishings, and other household operations and supplies.

2. **Transportation** equals $9,049 or 14.1% of after-tax income. Transportation includes vehicle purchases, related vehicle expenses, and gasoline, as well as public transportation.

3. **Food** accounts for $7,203 or 11.2% of after-tax income. Food consists of both eating at home for $4,049 and $3,154 spent on food eaten away from home.

4. **Health care** equals $4,612 or 7.1% of after-tax income. Health care includes health insurance, medical care and supplies, and prescriptions drugs.

5. **Entertainment** is $2,913 or 4.5% of after-tax income. Entertainment includes expenses in the home and outside of the home like going to the movies or concerts. It also includes any pet related expenses. Now readers, please don't get upset with me for calling your beloved Meow-zer or Lord Buffington an entertainment expense, blame the stern crew at BLS. Alcoholic beverages account for $484 per year which we will add to entertainment. This brings the total for entertainment spending to $3,397 or 5.2% of after-tax income.

As we total the five categories above, we see that the average household spends $43,147 or **67.2%** of their **$64,175** *after-tax* income on housing, transportation, food, health and entertainment. If these are the categories where most spending occurs, it is only natural that this is where you need to focus your attention to cut costs. Every dollar you save on spending frees up a dollar for investing and buys you a little more of your financial freedom.

For the rest of this chapter and in the next chapter we will look at ways to track spending and revise your spending habits with the specific goal of reducing your monthly spending by 25% or more in these five categories. Yes, that's right 25% or more. We will also discuss the risks related to credit card debt and explain strategies for paying off this debt.

Tracking Spending

An important first step on the path to financial freedom is tracking your spending every month. I know, I know, some people break out in hives at the thought of tracking expenses and budgeting, but it needs to be done and will pay so many dividends in the long run. We will break this process down into three parts to make it simple and we will start with the easiest part.

Part 1: Past Year of Spending

The first part is tracking your spending for the past year. Many credit cards and banks provide an annual summary of spending separated by category which you need, but you also need to look at the individual line item of each expense. You are looking for expenses that stand out as undesirable or excessive. You are also looking to understand your spending patterns. For example, do you make large cash withdrawals after you had a few beers and don't know where that money went. Or maybe you have a habit of excessive online shopping or collecting trinkets that have no real value. Perhaps you spend excessively at restaurants for lunch or you frequently order in for dinner. As you go through the statements you can put a + next to purchases you would make again and a - next to the ones that you prefer not to repeat.

This process is not intended to make you feel bad about your spending decisions, it is to help you better understand your spending habits and how they need to change. As you complete this exercise keep a list of all the spending habits you want to change and the specific type of expenses you will eliminate. There may be recurring monthly expenses you were not even aware of such as paying for an old gym membership. If you are billed for a monthly subscription service you don't need make the call today to end the service. If you are not sure if you still want the service, cancel it for a few months and see if you miss it. Often you won't, but if you do, try to find a less expensive alternative.

This one simple exercise may cut your spending by $200 to $1,000 per month. When you complete this exercise, you should have a budget sheet showing what you spent each month, in each category, for the past year. You will also have a list of the specific types of expenses and spending habits you hope to eliminate in the future. Keep this list posted somewhere that you can see it every morning. This is part of changing your money mindset.

Part 2: Track What You Spend

From today forward you will track what you spend and place it in one of your specific budget categories. You should have the five main budget categories from the last exercise for **housing** (including utilities and furniture), **transportation** (vehicles, gas, and public transportation), **food** (separated by what is eaten at home and outside of the home), **health care** and **entertainment** (including pet expenses and alcohol) and then add other categories such as clothing, gifts, credit card debt and interest payments, etc.

This is retrospective budgeting, and it will do two things. First, the process of watching more closely how you spend will lead you to spend less. This is similar to what we discussed in chapter 6 about tracking your real hourly rate, you tend to spend less the more you think about the impact expenses have on your personal finances. Second, this process will help you determine how much of your total after-tax income you are spending in each category.

The key for this to be successful is that you must track all spending including cash withdrawals; *every dollar goes under one of your categories and there is no miscellaneous category*. If you do not accurately track your expenses, you will be working from flawed data. The other key to make this successful is to set up a process for when you document your spending; it could be every evening or morning. If you do it infrequently like every week you are more likely forget and won't keep proper records. There are also many online budgeting tools if you prefer to automate the process.

Part 3: *What You Intend to Spend (Prospective Budget)*

After you have reviewed all your expenses for the past year and started a retrospective budget to track current spending, the third step is to create a forward-looking budget. This is a *prospective budget* for what you intend to spend in each category, each month, for the next year. Your prospective budget will list what you currently spend each month in your *current amount* column and what you plan to spend in your *budgeted amount* column.

You will have to make trade-offs and choices to ensure you keep within your spending limits. This is a process of relearning how to spend money. *You are literally retraining your brain to spend wisely.* Try to remind yourself that you are not buying a particular item today, because it will lead to some future benefit such as paying off your house in ten years or paying for a dream vacation. Keep what motivates you in the forefront of your mind to strengthen your skills of delayed gratification.

Prospective Budgeting is Temporary

Many people don't like adhering to a prospective budget, myself included, but they are necessary until you control your spending decisions. *If your spending consistently falls within your desired levels each month you can reward yourself by no longer creating prospective budgets.* But you will still want to keep a record of your retrospective spending each month. If you overspend again, you will need to go back to the prospective budget until you can keep your spending in line.

Example Budget Using BLS Data

Below is an example of a prospective budget using the BLS expense data for **Current Amount**. The **Budgeted Amount** is what you intend to spend and the difference is your **Savings** for each category.

Expense	Current Amount	Budgeted Amount	Savings
Housing	$1,574	$787	$787
Transportation	$754	$500	$254
Food	$600	$400	$200
Health	$384	$384	$0
Entertainment	$283	$180	$103
			$1,344

In the example above, only the top five categories of expenses are listed, but your budget will have more categories, such as clothing, electronics, education, and payments of credit card debt and interest. See the sample budget sheet in the *10 Stages Workbook*.

Savings Rate of 25%

You may be surprised at how much you can cut your monthly expenses. We will cover this in the next chapter, but cutting your spending by 25% or more is not as hard as you may think. It requires some short-term sacrifices, but the changes are relatively minor compared to the long-term benefits. And this example shows how cutting some of your five biggest expense categories can dramatically ramp up your savings. The person in this example would save $1,344 a month or $16,128 per year. Think about how much your money related stress would decline if you had $16,128 saved in just one year. Now compound that over a few years and you can see how financial freedom is possible.

As you become more skilled at creative cost cutting your savings rate may exceed 50% or more of your annual income. There are many years when we were saving more than 67% of our total after-tax income, while still maintaining the quality of life that we wanted. Reducing expenses and investing the savings creates the multiple income streams you need for financial independence and early retirement.

Health Spending Remains Constant

You will notice that the category of health was left the same without a reduction in health-related expenses. This is for three reasons. First, health care is often tied to employment and includes health insurance premiums which may be difficult to reduce in the short term. Second, some individuals are born with health issues that make it difficult to reduce their health care costs in a significant way. The strategies in this book do not exclude people just because of pre-existing health conditions. We created a plan that works for everyone, even if they face unique or expensive health issues.

Third, the cost of health care has been rising at a higher pace than other spending categories in the United States. Health care increased by 6.2% in 2016 according to the BLS survey. This trend has been happening for years and lower health care costs are unlikely in the future. In 2019 Fidelity Investments estimates that a retiring 65-year-old *couple* will need about $285,000 to cover their health care and medical expenses throughout retirement. This is a 78% increase from Fidelity's

2002 estimates. *Failure to adequately prepare for future health care costs is probably one of the greatest risks to a successful retirement.*

The next chapter will look at ways to help reduce health care expenses, but the key to curbing these costs is to engage in healthy habits such as regular exercise, quitting smoking/vaping, eating a proper diet, setting healthy sleep habits, and limiting your alcohol consumption. These practices are specifically addressed in the 70 tasks included in the *10 Stages Workbook*.

Key Takeaways:

•   On average 67.2% of a household's after-tax income is spent on housing, transportation, food, health care and entertainment.

•   If you monitor your spending more closely and take time to think before you make a purchase, you will reduce your spending and train your brain to make wise decisions on spending.

•   Tracking your spending for the past year will help you identify unnecessary purchases and spending habits that need to change. You can begin to cut monthly subscription services you don't use or other recurring expenses you can live without. Also look for less expensive alternatives, as every dollar you save takes you closer to financial freedom.

•   As you create a prospective budget and track every dollar you spend, you will be able to set spending targets for each category of your budget.

•   You can reduce your spending by 25% per month, primarily by cutting expenses in the five major categories of expenses, and you will invest these savings to create multiple income streams. Over time your annual savings rate can exceed 50% of your after-tax income. The more you invest the less dependent you become on your regular job.

CHAPTER 8: REDUCE LIVING EXPENSES BY 25% OR MORE

Lowering Housing Costs

Housing is likely to be your biggest monthly expense. Although having an apartment or house to yourself is nice, you need to recognize this choice incurs significant costs. The best way to cut housing expenses is to split housing costs with other people. If you have a roommate or two, you can divide the rent and the utilities and pay a smaller share. If you purchase a property and take on tenants as roommates, you will dramatically reduce your housing expenses while building equity in your home. Some people refer to this strategy as house hacking.

The first property I bought had a mortgage payment of $900 per month. After I brought in a roommate paying $550 per month, my share of the monthly payments fell to $350. I also cut my monthly utilities in half which freed up another $100 per month. I used the savings to fund my retirement account and to save for the down payment on my next property.

Bigger Property, Better Deal

If I had been more knowledgeable about real estate at the time, I could have been living for free. I bought a two-bedroom one-bathroom apartment, but for $30,000 more I could have bought an apartment in the same building with three bedrooms and two bathrooms. This apartment would have increased my mortgage and taxes by about $225 per month but would have allowed me to get a second roommate for an additional $550 per month. I could have reduced my share of the mortgage payment to $25 per month. *If you can purchase a three or four bedroom property with roommates who are tenants, you can lower your housing expenses to $0 or even make a monthly profit.*

Creative Rent Reductions and House Sharing

There are many ways to be creative in cutting your housing costs. In college, my roommates and I worked out a deal with our property manager to use our apartment as the model. In return for showing prospective tenants our place we received a $200 rent reduction each month. If you are skilled at making simple home repairs, you may be able to obtain free or reduced rent in an apartment building by responding to basic repairs for other tenants. Always look for these creative options to cut your housing costs.

If you don't want permanent roommates, consider using a home sharing site like Airbnb to temporarily rent out rooms or rent out your entire property when you are away. These services can help you lower your housing expenses while still retaining some privacy. What is important to remember is small inconveniences will have a massive payoff in the long run. *Your willingness to have roommates for several years or periodically rent out a room in your property could allow you to retire 15-20 years earlier; that is a pretty sweet trade.*

Duplex, Triplex or Fourplex

Families with kids are understandably more reluctant to have adults renting a room in their house, particularly if it is not a person they know. Another way to lower your housing costs is to purchase a duplex, triplex or fourplex property. The other units in the building will generate rents to pay your share of the mortgage while still retaining your privacy. If you have a family don't let buying a single-family home be your default decision. Just because most people do it does not mean it is a smart decision. We will cover the topic of investment properties in much more detail in the chapters on real estate.

Lowering Transportation Costs

Transportation is likely to be your second highest monthly

expense and these costs are closely tied to your housing situation. It is worth changing where you live if it significantly reduces your transportation costs. As part of the tasks in the *10 Stages Workbook* you will find a property that you can share with others to lower your housing expenses, so factor in proximity to work and public transport in this decision.

When I bought my first property, I chose it specifically because it was located next to a subway station. The proximity to the subway meant I did not need a car and the location appealed to renters who rely on public transportation. The property came with a designated parking space, which I did not need, so I could rent it for additional income. This extra $100 a month could pay all my utilities or go straight to savings. At the time, my employer also offered public transportation subsidies which reduced the expense of commuting to work by a few hundred dollars each month. Factor in these types of transportation savings options when you look for housing.

Factor in Stress with Transportation and Housing

Sitting in traffic congestion is probably the worst way to start and end your workday. I am always surprised by people's decision for a larger house far away from downtown, only to spend an hour in traffic each way. The commuting time lowers your hourly rate of income as we discussed in chapter 6 and reduces the amount of time available to enjoy this larger but distant home. Factor in the ability to walk or ride your bike to work when you choose a place to live. These are healthier and stress reducing options in addition to being cheaper. Personally, I use my morning commute of walking/biking to catch up on my favorite podcasts. This provides me with some exercise and as discussed in chapter 3 helps me learn something new every day to further our long-term goals.

Eliminate Your Car

Purchasing a car should never be your default decision. *A*

$30,000 car is equal to nearly 2,000 hours of work <u>after taxes</u> for a person making $40,000 a year. New vehicles depreciate immediately after you drive off the dealer's lot, leading to an instant financial loss. There are also all the associated costs of car ownership such as maintenance, tolls, new tires, insurance, repairs and any taxes or annual registration fees. According to NerdWallet the average cost of car ownership is $706 per month which is $8,469 per year. Many families own two cars and 35% of families own three cars, doubling or tripling these monthly expenses. *If you have an expensive car and are not yet financially free, seriously consider selling it.* If you must have a car use the proceeds of the sale to buy an inexpensive used car with a reputation for quality and resale value.

Choosing to live close enough to work will eliminate your need for a car and drastically reduce your transportation expenses. For the periods when you need a car you may find it is cheaper to use taxis or ride sharing services. You can also use rental cars when you want to leave town or need a car for an extended period. An appealing aspect of rental cars is getting the right vehicle for the task. If you are skiing, you rent a four-wheel drive, if you are traveling for several days you can rent a small camper van. The right car for the right job.

Reducing Food Expenses

When I started my first job, I was surprised to see that most of my colleagues went out to lunch every day instead of bringing lunch from home. I estimated that drinking coffee at work and bringing my lunch saved about $7 per day or $1,750 per year. To put it into another context, eating out for lunch every day is equal to approximately 112 hours of work <u>after taxes</u> for a person making $40,000 a year. *Think about that, you are working almost three weeks each year, just to pay for eating lunch at work.*

Paying $5 for gourmet coffee and $15 for lunch is a great way to work a job until you are well into your 70s. As the BSL data shows for the average household, food expenses consist of $4,049 for eating at home and $3,154 for food eaten away from home. The second category of $3,154 for food eaten away from home is where you want to focus your efforts.

Food from restaurants or convenience stores includes significant price mark-ups compared to food prepared at home. Eating food on the go also frequently leads to consuming less healthy options which can drive up future health expenses. *The key to cutting your food costs is to plan for the 21 meals you will eat each week, so you don't have to buy food at the last minute.* There are also options to clip coupons or buy in bulk at warehouse or discount grocery stores to lower your food bill.

There are many options for reducing your food expenses; you just need to find the ones that work best for you. It is important to emphasize that you are not just saving for the sake of saving; you are rechanneling this money to a higher and better use. Bringing your lunch to work for ten years and investing the difference could pay for your kid's college education or save the entire down payment for your retirement house. Again, it is small sacrifices that generate a huge long-term return. In our first jobs we brought our lunches from home every day for two years and used the savings for the deposit on an investment property. We traded lunch for a property that was a huge step towards financial freedom. Once you identify your priorities your money can begin working to achieve these long-term goals.

Reducing Health Expenses

Your ability to lower health care costs will depend on your level of pre-existing health conditions, coupled with your ability and willingness to engage in activities that support positive health. Regular exercise, healthful eating, reducing stress in your life, and getting adequate sleep are the key drivers for preventative health care. Expect health care costs in America to follow the trend of the past two decades and increase disproportionally compared to other expenses.

Rising health care costs are likely to be the greatest risk to your early retirement plans, especially if your budget can't absorb higher than expected expenses or a major health issue in the future. A serious illness can also deprive you of your ability to work, worsening an already difficult financial situation. You must plan for these risks as part of your early retirement strategy.

Tax Deductible Health Savings Account

A way to cut your health-related expenses is to set up an account that contributes *pre-tax dollars* for health-related expenses. In countries with public health care coverage like Australia, Canada and New Zealand future health care costs are lower and these types of tax deductible accounts are less common. In the United States individuals shoulder more of the burden of their health costs and there are two types of these tax deferred accounts.

The first is a Flexible Spending Account (FSA) for people who have health insurance, with a **low deductible**. The FSA allows you to set aside a few thousand dollars each year, tax free, to pay for medical expenses. One caveat with FSAs is the entire balance must be used before the end of the calendar year or else it is forfeited. Before opening an FSA account check with you employer or health insurance provider regarding your deductible level and the savings cap for an FSA.

The second type of tax deferred account is a Health Savings Account (HSA) which is for people who have a **high deductible** health insurance plan. An HSA allows you to save thousands of dollars to pay for health-related expenses. What distinguishes an HSA from an FSA is that HSA money can grow year after year as a form of tax deferred savings. It does not have to be used before the end of the year.

Employers are increasingly switching to high deductible health insurance plans because they are less expensive for the company to offer, so expect these plans to become more common. This is another example of employers shifting the cost of benefits to their employees. If you do not have a high deductible health insurance plan, still consider the FSA described previously.

Remember the amount you can save under each of these plans and the deductible levels change each year. You need to check the rules for the current year before opening an account. For more details please see the article on health expenses on LoadedforLife.com.

General Ways to Save on Health Expenses

For daily health expenses there are many ways to cut costs. Proper preventative care of your teeth can reduce the risk of cavities and future dental work. If you do need treatment, dental schools provide care by dental students at a reduced cost but don't worry, the procedures will be reviewed by a dentist.

If you receive medical treatment review every bill closely and challenge any errors. Mistakes are more common than you would expect. Also challenge any denial of payment for service from your insurance provider if you suspect a mistake. This requires research and closely reviewing your policy.

There are ways to look for generic drugs to reduce the cost of medicine including comparing prices at large discount stores or online. Some non-profit organizations such as NeedyMeds.org and Partnership for Prescription Assistance (pparx.org) may be useful resources. If any prescription drugs are being taken for an illness that could be significantly improved with diet and exercise, it is time to get serious about these issues to curb your costs and reduce your exposure to medicines which could potentially have negative side effects.

As you work through the *10 Stages Workbook* you will see that there are several specific tasks that are designed to help improve your long-term health and reduce your health-related expenses.

Reducing Entertainment Expenses

There are countless ways to reduce entertainment expenses without diminishing your social life. When we lived in Washington D.C., we took advantage of world class experiences for a fraction of the retail price. At the Shakespeare Theater we would purchase a deeply discounted ticket and stand at the back. During the intermission we could take one of the vacant seats for the rest of the performance. At one performance we sat a few rows behind a former U.S. President, poor guy paid too much for his seats.

We attended a small theater near our house where we would hand out programs to guests in exchange for watching the performance for free. This was a great way for the theater to cut its labor costs. We also bought a t-shirt at a local comedy club which allowed us to attend every Tuesday show for free. It was a slow night for the theater and the shirts drove more business.

We also found a range of impressive free speaker programs at local universities and through museums. Spend a little time on research and planning and you will find great entertainment at a discount which will allow you to channel the savings into your investments. In the 10 *Stages Workbook* you will have specific tasks to get you out of your comfort zone and expand your entertainment options.

Pet Related Expenses

The last chapter noted that the BLS data includes pet ownership as part of entertainment expenses. I am an animal lover but taking on the important responsibility of caring for a pet includes assuming substantial financial expenses. The ASPCA estimates that the first-year cost of pet ownership exceeds $1,270 for a dog and $1,070 for a cat, with ongoing average expenses per year of nearly $700 each. Adopting a pet from a shelter can help reduce these expenses and provides a caring home for an animal in need. One caveat to remember regarding pets is that they can limit your options for housing, as certain properties may not allow dogs or cats. But, for many people a pet is such an important part of their life it is well worth the expenses. Before you make such a major commitment of caring for a pet, be sure you can afford the responsibility.

Renting, Borrowing, and Buying Used

One final thought on lowering your monthly expenses is to look at renting, borrowing, or buying items used. Thrift stores have great items at a steep discount. Buying used is also better for the environment by keeping items out of a landfill. When I was waiter in college, I needed to buy a pair of black dress shoes. I found a slightly worn pair for $2 that sold new for $120. I paid less for my shoes than the sales tax on the new pair. I wore the shoes for three years waiting tables and used the $118 in savings to help pay for a trip to the Grand Canyon, a far more enjoyable experience than owning new shoes.

Key Takeaways:

• Implementing cost cutting options on housing, transportation, food, health care and entertainment expenses will help you convert 25% or more of your after-tax income into savings for investing. Over time these savings can grow to 50% or more of your income.

• Look at your housing and transportation expenses together because the solution to lowering your housing costs may also be the solution to your transportation expenses.

• The privacy of your own home or apartment might be nice but decide whether it is worth working another 15 or 20 years before you retire. You cannot implement the plan in this book and not address your core five highest expenses.

• As you create a plan for financial freedom, anticipate significantly higher health related expenses in the future. Health costs will be the Achilles heel for some members of the retire-early community.

• Open a Flexible Saving Account or a Health Saving Account to lower your health care costs.

• Look for ways to find free or discounted entertainment; they exist in every city or town.

• Make renting, borrowing or purchasing used items your first options instead of buying new.

CHAPTER 9: ASSETS, DEBT, AND CREDIT CARDS

Assets Generate Income

You will often see people include personal property such as cars or furniture as an asset. It shows the difference between what consumers think are assets and what investors think are assets. Items bought retail that depreciate immediately after purchase are not assets. Cars, furniture, clothes and the random array of collectables sold in gift shops are not assets, regardless of what the salesperson says. An asset generates bankable cash flow and is highly likely to appreciate. A rental property generating $200 in monthly cash flow or owning part of a business that pays you a percentage of the profits are both assets.

Saving 6 to 8 Times Your Annual Living Expenses

In the last chapter we talked about how reducing your expenses by 25% provides you with the savings you need to build your investment portfolio. Below is an example of how over a ten-year period these savings will help you purchase assets nearly six times your annual living expenses. I hope this example illustrates how much you can achieve each year from cutting expenses.

If you have an after-tax household income of $50,000 and you reduce your expenses by 25% you will be living on $37,500 and saving $12,500. This is equal to saving $1,042 a month. If you invest this $1,042 per month and earn 10% per year, you will have approximately $213,500 after ten years. This is equal to saving 5.6 times the $37,500 you live on.

If you were to save the majority of future raises (avoiding lifestyle inflation) you would be able to save eight or nine times your annual living expenses in just a decade. If you take it a step further and generate some side income which we will discuss in chapters 18 and 19, you can boost your savings to ten times your annual living expenses. With an aggressive savings rate you will get significantly closer to financial freedom in just ten years.

When you have a savings target of 25% of your income the process gets easier and you can obtain a savings rate of 30% or 40% without feeling like you are depriving yourself. There were many years where we saved 67% of our after-tax income by cutting our five key categories of expenses while still living the life we wanted to live.

One thing to remember is the lessons from chapter 4 on how inflation erodes your purchasing power over time. Your $37,500 in annual expenses will rise over time, after a decade it may be closer to $48,000. Keep this in mind when you set your savings targets.

Home an Asset? Compare Renting Versus Buying

There is a common debate on whether a primary residence is an asset or not. The answer usually depends on when you sell your home. A primary residence that you live in for a few years and then sell for a nice profit, after paying all the closing costs, was clearly an asset. Even if you sell the home at a loss, it was still an asset if the total cost of owning was cheaper than the total cost of renting for the same period.

For example, if you live in a home for five years and lost $5,000 on the sale, but renting for five years would have cost $8,000 more than owning the home, consider the $3,000 difference as your return. It may not be a great return over five years, but it was better than losing the extra $3,000 by renting.

When Renting is Preferable

Be very cautious buying a home to live in if the total mortgage and property tax payments are significantly higher than the rent for a similar property. Some buyers blindly think their home is a great investment, because it saves them from paying rent. But property ownership brings other expenses, like property taxes and maintenance, that renters don't pay. You may have been better off renting and investing the difference in another asset like stocks. The surefire way to turn your home into an asset is to have roommates that pay rent which covers most of your housing expenses or to buy a multifamily property that you live in and rent out the other units.

Bad Debt, Good Debt, and Risk

There are only two kinds of debt, good debt and bad debt. Good debt finances the purchase of assets that generate income. These debts include a business loan or a mortgage on an investment property. Bad debt, on the other hand, is debt used to acquire personal property such as cars, furniture, or other consumer products. The reason it is bad debt is twofold.

First, banks will only loan you so much money based on your income level. The more bad debt you incur buying consumer goods, the less good debt you can obtain to purchase assets. The bad debt crowds out good debt.

Second, bad debt does not provide any income and does not increase net worth. Income generated from assets bought with good debt increases both your income and your net worth, providing you with the ability to access more good debt. Each time you successfully use good debt, you are rewarded with the ability to take on more good debt.

For example, you could use $50,000 in bad debt to purchase a car or $50,000 in good debt to purchase an investment property generating $200 in monthly cash flow. A year later the car will have depreciated in value and may only be worth $40,000. The property will have generated $2,400 in rental profits, adding to your net worth and your ability to qualify for a loan to purchase your next investment property.

Good Debt Can Go Bad

One caveat about good debt is that it will only remain good debt if you don't become overleveraged. Carrying more debt than you can manage is being overleveraged. Take the time to understand downside risk and factor it into your investment decisions. Do not let a large amount of debt on one major investment put your long-term financial plan in jeopardy. Some investors try to make up for lost time by swinging for the fences on one huge deal, but this can be a disaster. Be careful that you don't put yourself in a position where the failure of one investment puts the rest of your assets in peril. One way to mitigate your risk is to work with partners. It is better to have 20% of an investment that you can manage than 100% of an investment that, if it were to fail, could cause you financial ruin.

Dangers of Credit Card Debt

Bad debt becomes worse if it comes in the form of high interest credit card debt. If you buy a $100 shirt with a credit card with a 24% interest rate and don't pay off the balance for a year, you will have paid $124 for the shirt. If you don't pay off the balance for another year, the shirt cost you $154.76. Credit card debt can quickly get out of control.

Total credit card debt in the United States is $931 billion and in 2017 the average household *with credit card debt* had a balance of $15,983 according to a NerdWallet. If the annual interest rate on these cards is 20%, the household would pay $3,196 in annual interest for the year. *Credit card debt can devastate your personal finance goals; interest payments provide no value other than raising the cost of previous purchases.*

Many households use credit cards in the event of emergencies and the high interest rates quickly become a burden. Being able to avoid credit card debt underscores the importance of getting your financial house in order. If an emergency occurs, you want to have cash set aside to pay the bills without resorting to credit cards which will drastically increase the cost of this emergency over time.

How to Pay Off Credit Card Debt

Start by no longer carrying credit cards with you and delink them from the payment options on your mobile device. Carrying credit cards creates temptation so remove the temptation and carry cash. The most efficient way to pay off credit card debt is to pay down the balance on the card with the highest interest rate. Then move to the card with the second highest interest rate and repeat the process. Close each account after you pay it off.

If you are more motivated by seeing the number of cards decline versus the total dollar amount, you can use the snowball approach made popular by Dave Ramsey which involves paying off the card with the lowest balance and then moving to the card with the next lowest balance. This approach may seem more rewarding, but the first option is smarter financially.

Another option is to consolidate all your credit card debt under a single debt consolidation loan and then close each credit card account. If you have good credit, this option will provide you with one monthly payment at a lower interest rate. *This option only works if you have the discipline to close the credit card accounts and not go back to excessive spending.* Otherwise your total debt will increase, and you will be in a worse situation.

Key Takeaways:

- Personal property including vehicles, furniture and other

personal property are not assets. Assets increase your net worth and produce a regular income stream like rental income or dividends.

• Cutting your expenses by 25% will allow you to have more than six times your annual living expenses after a decade, but with a little creativity and avoiding lifestyle inflation you will likely save eight to ten times your annual living expenses. Remember the lessons of saving 25 times your annual retirement income (also the 4% rule) discussed in chapter 4.

• Taking on debt only makes sense if you are buying an asset and not if you are buying consumer products. Bad debt will crowd out your ability to take good debt and hurt your ability to create income streams.

• Taking on high debt levels for assets can lead to financial ruin if you are not careful; take on partners in an investment to reduce your risk if necessary.

• Pay off credit card debts by paying off the card with the highest interest rate; consider loan consolidation if you have the self-discipline to not incur new credit card debt.

CHAPTER 10: STUDENT LOANS AND COLLEGE DEGREES

A 2017 Federal Reserve Survey of Economics and Household Decisionmaking (SHED) found that two-thirds of graduates with a bachelor's degree believe that their educational investment paid off. It is great that a majority were pleased with their decision. But this also implies that one-third of graduates don't think their degree was a good financial decision. If 33% of people think a college education was not a wise investment, perhaps this money could have been better spent. Although financial returns are not the only benefits of a college education, analyzing the cost/benefit analysis in financial terms is good place to start.

Return on Investment (ROI) of a Degree

In their College ROI Report PayScales lists colleges that provide the best value to help you in this decision. Drawing from PayScales data, Money magazine reported that the average 20-year return on obtaining a bachelor's degree after deducting the cost of tuition and other college expenses is approximately $225,000. That is in comparison to a person with only a high school diploma. The returns are higher for students who major *and work* in one of the STEM subjects (science, technology, engineering and math) and who attend universities that place an emphasis on STEM related degrees.

The ROI Report is focused on the first 20 years of earning, which does not account for the fact that some individuals tend to reach their highest earning years after their mid-40s which would show an even higher return on their education investment. This means the rate of return for those who select the right education could be even higher if they work into their 50s and 60s. Although since you purchased a book about creating financial freedom and retiring early, you may not be planning on working into your 60s which means you will have fewer years to obtain a return on your education investment.

As the data shows, a college degree can provide significant financial returns if you choose the right degree and work in your field, but it also requires properly managing your student debt. The cost of college has increased 213% in the last 30 years from $3,190 for a student enrolling at a public four-year institution in 1987 to $9,970 for the 2017 school year in inflation-adjusted dollars. This dramatic rise in tuition prices has placed a college education out of reach for many people and fueled a massive increase in student loan debt.

These figures are just for tuition and don't include other expenses such as room and board, books, and fees. In 2018 the average cost for a year of college (tuition, fees, housing, meals, books and supplies) at a public university was $25,000 and at a private university it was nearly $50,000. Over four years a degree will cost $100,000 at a public university and $200,000 at a private university. For a detailed explanation on strategies for saving for college, please see the article How to Pay for College on www.LoadedforLife.com.

Student Debt Exceeds $1.5 Trillion

Increasing college costs have caused total U.S. student loan debt to balloon to more than $1.5 trillion and many graduates are struggling with their payments. According to Nerdwallet the average student loan debt in September 2019 was $46,822, but there are two million people who owe at least $100,000 in student debt and the average law school graduate has $112,776 in debt. This excessive student loan debt can hinder your ability to qualify for loans to purchase assets that will advance your goals of financial freedom.

Remember your long-term goal is to stop trading your time for money, so even though a college degree may offer a good re-turn on investment, your primary focus is on building income streams that will lead to financial independence, so manage your debt accordingly. Be sure to analyze your expected post-degree salary to ensure the degree is worth both the investment of time and money. You don't want the unpleasant surprise after you graduate of finding out the salaries in your field are not what you expected.

Increase Your ROI on a Degree

Like any investment you can improve your return on invest-ment (ROI) on a college degree by reducing your expenses and minimizing your future debt. Applying for scholarships and financial aid are the most definitive ways to reduce college ex-penses. There are niche scholarships for students who worked as a golf caddy, or have excellent shooting skills, or are the child of a former U.S. Marine. There are a number of small scholar-ships that can be layered to reduce your college expenses. I had a classmate who earned a full scholarship for her first two years of study. She cleverly took additional classes and went to summer school to cram three years of study into two years. It was not easy, but it saved her an entire year of college expenses.

Another way to reduce college expenses is by taking College-Level Examination Program (CLEP) tests while in high school which can provide college credit for a full course. Some ad-vanced placement classes in high school also provide college credit. Studying accredited courses online or attending a com-munity college for your first two years and transferring to a four-year institution will also significantly reduce the cost of a college education. You will obtain the same degree from the university whether you attended for four years or only two.

Working part-time while in school is a great way to reduce your need for loans and get some practical work experience. I knew a classmate who studied full-time for two years, then dropped back to one class each semester for two years to work selling luxury cars. His strategy was to make himself more competitive than other graduates by having two solid years of sales experience. He also saved enough while selling cars to graduate debt free.

When to Take Student Loans

There are advantages to taking student loan debt, if used correctly. When I was in law school, I took about $19,000 in student loans at a 3% interest rate. This freed up $19,000 to invest in real estate and avoid mortgage rates that were near 6%. Another strategy is finding employers who will pay back some of your student loans. My wife and I both had employers who paid for part of our degrees or repaid some of our student loans. This will significantly reduce the cost of your education.

If you have various debts including credit cards, mortgages, and student loan debt, *do not prioritize paying off student loans*. The interest may be tax deductible and an employer will not pay off credit card debt or mortgages, but they might pay off part or all of your student loans.

Degrees May Not Be the Way to Learn

There is some truth to the criticism that college teaches people how to be employees, not to be entrepreneurs or to create wealth. You could spend four years and $100,000 to earn a business degree in a classroom. However, if you already have some proven business savvy and have taken core business courses online, you could spend the same $100,000 launching a business.

In this situation it may make more sense to bring on some partners so you don't have to finance the venture on your own. The experience of starting a business is a remarkable education and even if the business ultimately fails, you have gained an education that is more practical than what you would learn in a classroom. Both forms of education have a price, the question is which one is a better fit for you and your approach to learning. We will cover this subject in more detail in the chapters on entrepreneurship, small business, and side hustles.

Apprenticeships and Mentoring

Another alternative to a college education is finding a person at a point in their career where you eventually want to be and offer to work for them for free or near free. Making a commitment of at least a year is going to make the offer more interesting to your potential mentor. As you approach them don't just ask them to mentor you. Research their business and see how you can provide value and use that as your entry point. If you are particularly good at social media and marketing, provide them with specific examples of what you can do to help grow their business. *Use the knowledge you have to get the knowledge you need.* If you are seeking to be paid, let them know you only want a percentage of the business you will bring to the company. You will therefore only be a source of profit and not an expense.

You may have to secure some savings in advance to use this strategy and perhaps take on some debt, but much less debt than required for a college degree. You could also work side jobs to make ends meet, but a year at the shoulder of an expert in your chosen field would be a priceless education and provide a network of contacts.

If you are considering a career in specific field and can't work for free for a year, look for opportunities to educate yourself about the career through entry level positions that don't require a degree. This is like taking a low-cost test drive in a career before committing to an expensive degree. You may also discover that a degree or at least the degree you were considering is not necessary. A Federal Reserve Bank of New York study found 44 percent of recent college graduates are underemployed and working in positions where their degree was not a prerequisite. A career test drive is a great way to avoid early mistakes in career choices. It is better to find out you don't like working in marketing, computer science, or accounting before you spend four years studying it as your major.

Wait Until Circumstances Improve

When I was finishing college, I planned to go immediately to law school. But when I ran the numbers, I realized the degree would put me $80,000 in debt. I feared being locked into practicing law to pay off this debt regardless of whether I liked being a lawyer. Such a huge amount of debt would also limit the ability to travel, so I shelved my plans for law school.

Fortunately, this decision opened the door to joining the Peace Corps and meeting my wife. When I did decide to go to law school I went at night while working full-time. It is far more challenging to balance work with being a full-time student, but it dramatically reduced my need for school loans. And as mentioned earlier, my employer paid back most of this student loan debt. My lack of debt also gave me the freedom to skip being a lawyer and accept an offer to move to Lebanon. Timing your education in a way that retains flexibility and limits debt will prevent you from regretting the expense.

You are now ready to start <u>Stage 1</u> of the *10 Stages Workbook* available on www.LoadedforLife.com.

Key Takeaways:

• A college education may be a wise investment, but it depends on your long-term career plans. Loading up on student debt could restrict your ability to pivot in your career and could lock you into a career you don't enjoy, at least for a few years.

•   Test out your chosen career path in an entry level position that doesn't require a degree or advanced degree before you commit to an expensive education.

•   There are options to get career experience without a degree as well as creative ways to help cover the costs of a college education without taking on significant debt.

•   Consider working for an expert in the field for free or near free for a year, but be prepared to show them how you can add value to their business when you approach them with the offer.

•   Student loan debt can be beneficial because employers may pay for part of your degree or repay your student loans. Pay student loan debt back last, because employers won't repay your mortgage or credit card debt.

•   For a detailed explanation on saving for college please see the article How to Pay for College on www.LoadedforLife.com.

•   Start work on Stage 1 of the *10 Stages Workbook* available at www.LoadedforLife.com.

CHAPTER 11: REGULAR JOBS: LESSONS NOT TAUGHT IN SCHOOL

We learn many valuable skills in school, but wealth creation and being entrepreneurial with our money are not necessarily among them. Unfortunately, the traditional advice of study hard and get a well-paying job still prevails in education. Incorporating discussions about the benefits and drawbacks of regular jobs would be tremendously beneficial in helping young people prepare for future careers. It might encourage more students to take risks and follow their passions by considering entrepreneurship as a first option. It would also serve to reassure students who are not cut out for traditional classroom learning that there are other paths to success in life that match their talents. Below are some lessons about traditional employment that schools don't teach which should help you avoid job-related pitfalls and improve your chances of achieving financial freedom.

Employees Are Pushed Out of Jobs in Their 50s

In the last chapter we talked about how your salary may be highest when you are in your 50s or 60s. While these may be your high earning years, a recent study by ProPublica and the Urban Institute found that 56% of older workers are pushed out of their longtime jobs well before they expected. Unfortunately, many of these older workers had planned to use these high-income years to play catch up on their retirement savings. The study also found that only 10% of older workers who lose their jobs find new jobs that match their previous salaries.

You can't wait to save for your retirement until you are in your 50s because the job market becomes less stable. You may lose the high salary you were counting on to save for retirement. Losing your job in your 50s and 60s and returning to the market at a lower wage means you will be working much longer than previously planned.

This is one of the reasons we are seeing more workers working into their 70s or even 80s. In addition, if you face health complications later in life it may limit your ability to work, making a bad situation worse. *Recognize that you could be laid off, transferred or forced to accept lower pay when you are in your 50s and take steps now to protect yourself.*

Two-Thirds of Workers Don't Like Their Jobs

I would have been shocked as a student to learn so many people don't like their jobs. It is not really a subject that is discussed in school. Yet, a 2017 Gallup study found 51% of full-time employees said they have no real or meaningful connection to their jobs and tend to do the bare minimum. Another 16% are actively disengaged and resent their jobs. We are talking about millions and millions of people in this situation. This is tragic and helps explain why there are such high levels of stress. The high numbers of people worried about money combined with the large percentage of people who don't like their jobs indicates a crisis in society.

Creating your financial plan is a way for you to take back some control and to help you find fulfilling work while insulating yourself from being stuck in a meaningless job. If you don't like your job you will have other income streams to pay your bills while you find something better. You may find that the type of work you want to do in your 20s or 30s changes, and changes again in the decades that follow. If you no longer enjoy your job and feel trapped, this sense of unease will create stress that permeates into other areas of your life. Over time it will have a negative impact on your personal relationships, home life, and health.

Durable Exit Strategy

One of the most important lessons of this book is to understand the concept of building a durable exit strategy from your day job. You never know what will happen to your job or to your employer. Your business could run into financial trouble, a horrible boss could replace your excellent boss, or a competitor may acquire your company and eliminate your position. Many things can happen that are outside of your control, so manage what is within your control, which is your money/investments and continuously improving your skills to remain competitive. Building a durable exit strategy begins from your very first job and should continue throughout your career.

A well-designed durable exit strategy affords you the financial cushion and the flexibility to make career course corrections. You can avoid being among the bored worker statistics by chasing what excites you in a deliberate, focused, and sustained manner. Make no mistake, this doesn't mean it will be easy. There will be periods when work is good and bad, but having options and staying agile will make you happier and wealthier. *Your work should provide you with opportunities for thrills, skills, and profits.* If work becomes tedious, you need to think about how you can pivot to get back on a better path. The Bureau of Labor Statistics reports that a person will have 12 jobs in their career, that is a lot of pivoting in life.

Benefits Outweigh Salary

Before you accept a job, spend time asking questions about the benefits. Often people only look at the salary and forget that benefits can be far more valuable. As discussed in Chapter 5 your income will be subject to multiple taxes, but benefits are usually not taxed. If you have a job that offers free housing, public transportation subsides or educational allowances, these are far more valuable than the cash equivalent because they are not taxed. Look closely at the benefits because that is where the real value rests for jobs and can outweigh another job offer with a higher salary.

Beware of Golden Handcuffs

Pay attention to this section because this is such a common mistake and the penalties for this mistake is severe. Before you accept a job, make sure you understand how many years it takes before you become eligible for key benefits. For example, it may take decades to become a partner in the business or to receive equity in the business, or before you become eligible for certain retirement benefits. People neglect to assess these benefits because they seem so far in the future. There are two reasons why accepting a job without evaluating these benefits is risky.

First, the rules can change the day before you acquire the benefits and you will forfeit the preceding years for a reduced benefit or no benefits at all. *Don't fool yourself as this has happened to countless workers over the years and continues to happen every day. It can definitely happen to you.* If your employer gets into financial trouble you could lose the benefits you have been counting on for years. Look up the stories of people who worked for their entire careers and lost everything when the business failed. If your company is bought by a competitor your benefits could be slashed. The worst is when employees see their retirement benefits or pensions reduced when they are older and have little time to make up for the loss.

The second reason not assessing delayed benefits is so risky is that you may decide after several years that you are ready to move on but will lose the benefits if you leave early. This puts you in the unenviable position of forgoing a significant financial benefit or riding out the additional years in a job you prefer to leave. This is what it means to be trapped in golden handcuffs. To protect yourself, look for employment where the benefits mature at periodic stages along the way. This allows you the flexibility to leave when you decide you are ready. One cannot go back in time to reverse the decision of choosing an employer, so it important to weigh all these options before accepting these types of positions.

Is Seeking Promotions Wise?

For many people the way of increasing their income is by being promoted and climbing the career ladder. This encourages people to channel most of their efforts into seeking promotions instead of pursuing investment opportunities. This is not necessarily an efficient process and may lead to a relatively low rate of return on the amount of time and effort invested. It also results in pursuing the type of income that will be taxed at higher rates instead of lower taxed income from investments.

Even those who truly love their jobs and are not particularly worried about promotions should recognize that securing financial freedom is about making efficient decisions related to time, effort, and income. There is also the risk that promotions are not allocated in an equitable manner. Like most people, I have seen people win promotions they didn't deserve because of office politics or stealing credit for work they didn't do. This is just part of working life, but these inefficiencies in the system of promotions can negate the return on your efforts.

Measuring the Value of the Promotion

My friend Sharon provides a perfect example for how to calculate the value of promotions. Where Sharon works all the employees at her level compete once a year for a limited number of promotions. A promotion would add $10,000 to Sharon's salary and she thinks she has a 50% chance of being promoted. One way to measure the value of a reward like a promotion is to multiply the reward by the likelihood it will occur. Hence a 50% chance of receiving a $10,000 promotion means the promotion is worth $5,000. This assumes there are no additional non-financial perks that come with the promotion that would make it more valuable. Sharon said if she is not promoted this year, she gets no increase in salary, and must wait until next year to compete in the next round of promotions.

Measure the Cost of the Effort

Now that we know Sharon's promotion has a value of $5,000, the second step is to calculate the value of her extra effort to get the promotion. We calculate the effort in terms of the number of additional hours Sharon plans to work hoping it will get her promoted. In chapter 6 we learned the methods for calculating your real per hour income rates. Sharon had done the math and knows she makes $50 per hour. Sharon divides the estimated benefit of $5,000 by her hourly rate of $50 and arrives at 100 hours.

Apply the Effort to Match the Benefit

If Sharon is thinking in terms of maximizing her efficiency, she should not commit any more than 100 hours of additional effort this year to obtain the promotion. If she thinks promotions are becoming scarce and she only has a 10% chance of being promoted, the value of the promotion is only $1,000 and she should only apply 20 hours of additional effort to get it. She could work more hours, but it would be an inefficient use of her time because the promotion is not worth it. Instead Sharon could spend these hours more wisely by pursuing other investments or a side business with a higher return.

Don't Overvalue Benefits

Some of you might be thinking that Sharon's extra effort will be noticed by her employer which improves the likelihood of future promotions, even if she is not promoted this year. This strategy might work for Sharon, but that strategy is a gamble, not a calculated investment of time in return for a reward. It is also thinking like an employee, not an investor and tends to make people overvalue promotions. *Our goal is to calculate the value of a reward in definite terms, so we can make the optimal choice for maximizing the return on our efforts.*

Sharon can't bank on the good will of her employer; her boss may change, and the new boss won't know of her efforts or her office may downsize and there are no promotions. There are too many factors at play that could diminish the value of her extra work as she waits another year for the next round of promotions. At some employers promotions are directly tied to reaching specific goals making them more merit based, but that is not the case for Sharon; she is relying on a review of her overall performance by a selection of senior staff. The ability to control being promoted is mostly out of her hands.

You may also think Sharon's promotion should be valued at more than $5,000 because the higher salary will carry into future years. Again, this is falling into the trap of over valuing the promotion. Sharon may not stay with the employer or the employer may begin layoffs in the future or need to make salary reductions. The future value of the promotion is uncertain, so she should not factor it in to her calculations or else she will again overvalue the promotion and put too many hours into getting it than it is worth.

Don't Confuse Hours Worked with Value Created

Before we move off this subject, I want to be clear on a few points to put the previous section into context. Using this tool to value promotions is about maximizing your efficiency. You are valuing your time and assessing a value on what your employer is potentially offering in the form of rewards so you can make informed decisions.

The relationship you have with your employer can't simply be broken down to just hours worked, you are also looking at the value you bring to the employer and your emotional connection to the employer. You always want to give your employer your very best performance while on the job and stand out for the quality of your work, not for the quantity of hours worked.

In addition, you may also be working for a company that has treated you exceedingly well in the past, but has hit a rough patch and you are personally committed to giving them extra time regardless of the pay because you believe in their mission and you want to help them survive. Just keep these factors in mind as you internalize this section.

As we discussed in chapter 6, when calculating your per hour income rate, the more hours you work for the same salary, the more you dilute your hourly rate of income. Don't try to cheat your employer by working fewer hours, but also don't cheat yourself by working so many additional hours that you water down your salary. Find the balance of creating value for the employer and a reasonable hourly rate for yourself which provides adequate time for other priorities in life. It is easy for people to get consumed by their jobs, you want to take a step back and make measured decisions about jobs, promotions, and work/life balance.

Investments Are More Efficient than Promotions

Next, we are going to take what we learned about Sharon, calculating the value of a promotion to compare promotions to other opportunities to create wealth which may have a better return. You will find that chasing promotions is often not the optimal use of your time. Allocating the same number of hours to an investment can both increase the certainty of the return and be more lucrative.

Promotions = Power in Their Hands

We know Sharon is looking at spending 100 hours to secure a promotion valued at $5,000. There is only one way to get this reward which is getting promoted. This process is out of Sharon's hands as those approving the promotions make the decision. Sharon's control and influence are very limited. Sharon also only gets one chance at a promotion each year; if she is not promoted, she must wait until next year for the next promotion round. However, if Sharon chose to skip working an extra 100 hours trying to get promoted, she could use this time to find and buy a rental property. This approach puts more of the decision-making power in her hands and creates at least three ways that she could secure the hoped-for reward of $5,000 that a promotion would have provided.

Investments = Power in Your Hands

Sharon is looking for a $100,000 rental property and there are three ways she could earn the desired $5,000. First, she could negotiate the purchase price of the property down to $95,000. It is not tremendously difficult to find a motivated seller willing to reduce the selling price of a property by $5,000 or more. If a seller says no, Sharon can move on to find a more motivated seller.

Second, Sharon can buy a property that needs some minor renovations which, once completed, would increase the value of the property by $5,000 or more. Adding new paint, a new front door, minor improvements in curb appeal and updating countertops and hardware in the kitchen and bathrooms can easily add $5,000 in value above the cost of the improvements. Again, the control in creating wealth is back in Sharon's hands. She is not waiting on an employer to decide her future, she is taking matters into her own hands.

Third, Sharon could generate the $5,000 in desired income from the monthly cash flow and equity earned from the property. If Sharon's property generates $417 per month in combined cash flow and equity, this will provide her with $5,004 for the year. As the years pass and she pays off the property her equity payments will increase beyond $5,004 adding to her net worth. She may also be able to raise the rent, further increasing her income. Best of all, if Sharon changes employers, she keeps this income stream. Sharon is creating multiple incomes streams and creating a durable exit strategy for herself from her day job.

Creating $5,000 at All Three Steps

If Sharon is diligent, she could:

1. Negotiate the property down by $5,000;

2. Fix it up to create $5,000 in value and;

3. Create $5,000 in cash flow and equity from the rents.

This approach has earned Sharon $15,000 in value by choosing to spend 100 hours buying a rental property versus chasing a promotion. In Chapter 5, we discussed how earnings from a promotion are active income which are taxed at a higher rate than the income from investments. Sharon will pay less tax on her rental property income than she would on the active income earned from a promotion.

Think Like an Investor, Not an Employee

The first key lesson here is to think like an investor versus an employee. *As an investor you create the value, you don't wait for someone to give it to you.* You are not relying on the good graces of others to see your talents and reward you. Employment is not always a meritocracy and you will not always be fairly rewarded for your performance. Think of all the people you know who get passed over for a promotion after putting in hours of extra work for their employer and making personal sacrifices. How do they feel afterwards? They usually feel cheated or resentful, which also makes them feel powerless. Even if you love your job and don't really care about promotions, you still want to allocate your time efficiently by focusing your efforts on building lasting income streams.

Stop Exchanging Time for Money

The second key lesson from Sharon's example is that employees think about trading their time for money, while investors seek to create income that doesn't require a corresponding amount of time. Income from rental properties, or from being a part owner in a business, or interest from bonds or dividends from stocks don't require a set amount of your time. They may require time, but it is not a specific amount of time for a specific amount of money. For example, as you grow your wealth you may spend 20 hours a month managing your rental properties that generate more income than you once earned in a job working 160 hours per month. This is how you stop trading time for money.

Treat Wages as Finite

One way to help you think like an investor is to treat the wages from your job like they are temporary and finite. Remind yourself that you only plan to work for a salary for a set number of years and then this income will stop. It will motivate you to convert as much of your salary as possible into other income streams. If your mindset is to be an employee forever, then you will. You want to think like an investor who has the financial freedom to leave their day job behind.

Key Takeaways:

•   We learn many helpful skills in school, but investing, wealth creation and how to be entrepreneurial are not among them.

•   Workers in their 50s have a 56% chance of being forced out of their current job, which could devastate their plans to save for retirement. Only 10% of older workers who are laid off ever return to their previous salary level and will likely have to work for many more years than intended before they can retire.

•   Nearly two-thirds of people don't like their jobs, and many try to get by doing the bare minimum, this is not a recipe for a happy and fulfilling life. Look for ways to pivot in your career so you can chase your passions.

• If you are looking at a possible promotion, use the tools we discussed to calculate its value so you can be efficient in the number of hours you commit to securing this benefit.

• Be very cautious of a job that offers benefits such as equity or a pension that don't mature for decades. The business could fail, and you will lose these benefits. Also, after several years you may no longer like this type of work or your employer, but you are trapped in golden handcuffs.

• Regular employment will help you jumpstart your goals of financial freedom, but it is still trading time for money. To become wealthy and build a durable exit strategy you need to think like an investor.

• Employment is not always a meritocracy and your effort are not always rewarded through promotions. Channel your efforts into investments that create revenue streams to replace your salary.

• Remember Sharon found three ways to make the desired $5,000 by putting control in her hands with real estate instead of waiting or hoping for a promotion from her employer.

CHAPTER 12: CREATING WEALTH

You are unlikely to become truly wealthy through earning a salary alone. Real wealth comes from investments that create income streams, usually taxed at a lower rate, which allows you to keep more of what you earn. The path to real wealth frequently comes from starting a profitable business that generates more revenue than you could ever make in a traditional job. One of the goals of a business is to replace yourself with talent so you can free up your time. You must keep an eye on the business to ensure that standards remain high, but to be successful the business needs to be able to run without your immediate presence.

Wealth also comes from creating a product, service or process that becomes intellectual property to be licensed or sold. The process to create the item or system requires a large time commitment, but once completed it will continue to pay revenue for years without the same initial time commitment. Even if your first efforts at creating a product or service fail, you will gain valuable experience for your next attempt.

Part of creating wealth is also knowing when to quit, recognizing that a concept or business is not viable so you can move on to the next idea before you put good money in after bad. We will cover this subject more in the chapters on entrepreneurship, side hustles, and small business.

Another way to create wealth is to add value to an investment, such as renovating a property. In one of our first real estate deals we bought a studio apartment and converted it into a one-bedroom apartment. We rented it for a few years and then sold it. We probably spent a total of 80 hours on this property the entire time we owned it. For those two weeks' worth of work we made a return of over $100,000. *Put simply, that is how you cre-*

ate wealth. You are creating value, not trading your time for a finite amount of salary. You need to recognize that your efforts in certain activities will yield remarkably higher returns than others.

One of the foundations for creating wealth is using the power of compounding interest that we discussed in Chapter 4. On the television show Shark Tank, investor Kevin O'Leary has said treat your money like an army that goes off to capture other monetary soldiers. Each dollar is expected to go out and bring back more of its peers. A $100 invested for a year earning 10% becomes $110. Let the dollars go out again for another year to earn 10% and it will become $121. This progressive expansion leads to exponential growth and sustainable wealth. *Creating wealth is not a sprint, it is a series of small steps each day that over the years makes success inevitable.*

Recessions and Depressions Create Wealth

Most people think that you create wealth when the economy is doing well, and it may appear that way initially. But if the boom is followed by a bust, which it usually is, a certain percentage of people will lose their jobs and assets. So, their wealth was only temporary. This often occurs when you let lifestyle inflation take over. In good times people fail to buy assets that create income or increase their savings and they instead live on credit and purchase luxuries. A significant amount of money changes hands during recessions. The people with enough cash ride through the downturn acquiring more assets, coming out wealthier after the recession. If you understand this lesson you end up being wealthier and if you don't, you are probably the one giving up the assets.

For example, during the 2007-08 global financial crisis properties that once sold for $300,000 fell to $140,000. People who had cash and available credit bought these properties at a discount and rented them. Fast forward ten years and the properties have appreciated to $300,000 again. If the buyer used a

15-year mortgage and rented the property, their tenant would have paid off two-thirds of the mortgage. The buyer now owns a property with a small mortgage with more than $250,000 in equity. She also continues to receive the monthly rental income. In five more years, the property will be paid off.

An important thing to remember is that the buyer could have bought this $140,000 property with a 20% down payment of $28,000. Which means she has turned an investment of $28,000 into more than $250,000. If you did this strategy five times you would have a net worth of $1,250,000. If the rental income from each of the five properties after expenses is $700 per month, the annual income is $42,000. *This is how millionaires are created, it is that simple.* The process is about buying at the right time, being able to hold through the downturn, and then paying down the debt. If you diligently complete all the tasks in the *10 Stages Workbook*, you can become the person buying these properties in the next economic downturn, *not the person selling.*

Plan to Hold Forever

Most of your investments should be in assets you intend to hold forever. If you buy stocks, they should be shares in companies you are hoping to never sell. If you buy rental properties or start a business, make investments you plan to hold for your entire life and then pass on to your heirs or favorite charity. Following this rule will reduce your tendency to jump into fad investments or try to time the market for a quick profit. *If you don't wish to own the investment in ten to twenty years, maybe you should not buy it today.*

There are a few exceptions to this rule which apply to investments that by their very nature are short-term. If you are skilled at renovating and selling houses, your business is based on a short hold period. But you should keep a portion of these properties as buy and hold investments to provide a long-term income stream. Flipping houses is still a job, the money stops when you stop working, unless you create a flipping business that can operate without your daily involvement.

Get a Partner When You Pivot

Bring in an experienced partner for your first deal if you are branching into a new area of investing. For example, if you switch from investing in single family properties to commercial properties, align yourself with someone you trust who has already had some success with commercial properties. Our tendency to do well in one investment class can make us overconfident when investing in a new asset class. There will be potential pitfalls with this new investment that you are unaware of and these mistakes can be expensive. Be willing to give up part of the deal to an experienced partner so you can learn and hedge the downside risk. Keep this quote in mind from Will Rogers, "*I am concerned more about the return of my money than the return on my money.*"

Capital is a Coward

One of my favorite quotes by former Secretary of State General Colin Powell is, "*Capital is a coward. It flees from corruption and bad policies, conflict and unpredictability. It shuns ignorance, disease, and illiteracy. Capital goes where it is welcomed and where investors can be confident of a return on the resources they have put at risk. It goes to countries where women can work, children can read, and entrepreneurs can dream.*"

I like this quote for many reasons. It goes back to my point in the Introduction about the importance of having enforceable contracts, property rights and access to credit which allow both a country and entrepreneurs to become successful. It is also a reminder to make sure you only invest with people who have integrity. If you treat people well and align their interests with your own, capital will find its way to you. *Sustainable wealth comes from treating capital well, both yours and your partner's.*

Don't Invest with Scared Money

General Powell's quote also makes me think about the risk of investing with scared money. If you borrow money make sure it is from someone who can stomach short-term volatility or setbacks with the investment. If your capital comes from a person who will nervously call you on a regular basis asking about the status of the investment, you will regret accepting their money.

Investing with scared money is not just about partners, it also applies to you. If you make an investment and then lay awake at night fretting, it was not the right investment for you. In the future you need to either take a smaller percentage of the deal or find a smaller deal that matches your comfort level. Each person has a certain risk tolerance when it comes to investing. Recognize and respect what your risk tolerance is so you can invest in a way that creates wealth but minimizes the stress in your life.

Build a Team of Experts

If you are looking to invest in real estate you will need a good realtor, property manager, and contractors who provide quality work for a fair price. You will also need a lender who is responsive and knowledgeable. As your investments become more complex you may need a tax advisor, a lawyer, and possibly an accountant for professional advice. The key to success is asking and paying these people for their advice before you implement a decision. It is nearly impossible for you to become an expert in all these subjects, so find talented people and build your team. Highly talented people tend to run in the same circles. Your realtor may be the lead to an excellent lender or amazing contractor. Leverage each relationship to find the next expert you need.

Highly talented people often charge a premium. They know they are better than their competitors and can charge more.

When dealing with highly talented people don't try to nickel and dime them on their fees, they will soon tire of working with you. Pay them promptly and be the client whose call they want to take. If you build the right team it will make each member of the team wealthier.

◆ ◆ ◆

Key Takeaways:

•   Traditional jobs will rarely make you wealthy; you need investments that generate income without a corresponding time commitment.

•   Starting businesses, creating products, services or processes that become intellectual property can create long-term income streams.

•   Real wealth is created during recessions when assets change hands. This is when millionaires are made. You want to be the one buying the assets, not selling them in a recession.

•   Plan to hold your investments forever; it will protect you from chasing fads or trying to time the market.

•   Get a partner if you are investing in a new asset class, as there are many things you may not know, and it is better to avoid mistakes by bringing in an experienced partner to help you. It is better to have a small part of a deal that makes money than all of a deal that loses money.

•   Capital is coward, treat it well if you want to create sustainable wealth. Remember not to invest with scared money, including your own.

•   Create a team of experts to help you. When investing in real estate you need a good realtor, lender, property manager and contractor. Truly talented people charge a premium and they are worth it.

CHAPTER 13: THREE TYPES OF INCOME AND THREE BUDGETS

This chapter will cover three types of income streams earned at different ages in life as well as three types of budgets you will need to fund for financial freedom. This information is the foundation for the next several chapters of the book, so it is worth a closer read.

Immediate Income

As you think about the income streams that provide financial freedom you will notice that some income becomes available at certain periods in your life. First is income you earn that is immediately available to you at any age without restriction or tax penalty. This might be the cash flow from a rental property or dividends earned from owning stocks in a non tax deferred account. It is also the income you receive from a full or part-time job. This is your *Immediate Income*, you earn it, and it is immediately yours to use for paying expenses or reinvesting.

Middle Age Income

The next category of income is *Middle Age Income*. This is income you earn from investments locked away in a tax deferred retirement account until you reach middle age. If you access these funds early you will usually pay a penalty and additional taxes. These are investments in retirement accounts like a 401(k) or an Individual Retirement Account (IRA). In the United States you can typically access these accounts at age 59½. We will discuss these retirement accounts in detail in chapter 16.

The key point to keep in mind is that your savings in these retirement accounts is not be available to you until you reach middle age. If you want to retire very early don't have all of your savings in these retirement accounts. Fortunately, there are a few ways to access these funds earlier than age 59½. which we will discuss later. You might be thinking, why don't I just focus on creating Immediate Income to avoid any restrictions on my money. The reason is you are able to avoid paying taxes now on the income you contribute to these retirement accounts. Using tax deferred retirement accounts is an excellent way to significantly lower your current taxes and increase the amount you can save because these accounts usually benefit from employers matching your contributions. If you save $10,000 and your employer has a 50% match you will have earned $5,000 just by using this tax deferred account. This is a great way to earn free money.

If you are planning on retiring in your late 50s, the income derived from these accounts can often be enough to eliminate your need for full-time work. Although you may still want to continue working part-time or develop a side hustle to retain social networks or focus on an aspect of work you enjoy most. In the next few chapters we will introduce a range of investments to help generate both *Immediate Income* and *Middle Age Income* and discuss the pros and cons of side hustles.

Senior Income

The last income category is *Senior Income*; this is the income you receive as a senior citizen from government superannuation programs or public pensions like Social Security Retirement Benefits. Each country has its own version of these programs for senior citizens but some are more generous than others. There are also ways to be strategic in accessing these accounts to maximize your benefits. For example, if you rely on your *Middle Age Income* and delay taking Social Security Retirement Benefits from age 67 to age 70 you can increase your monthly benefits by 24%. This is a way to increase your *Senior Income*, especially if you are in great health and longevity runs in your family.

One word of caution, people tend to overestimate their Social Security benefits and are frequently surprised to learn they can't live on their monthly payments alone. It will be your responsibility to investigate these benefits in your country as part of the *10 Stages Workbook*. In chapter 17 there is a detailed explanation of Social Security Retirement Benefits and ways to use annuities to create additional *Senior Income*. What is important to know for now is that you will not receive *Senior Income* until you are in your mid-60s or early 70s. So, if you are planning on retiring early this income will not be available to you for many years. There is also the possibility that these benefits will be reduced by governments in the future, a topic we cover in detail in chapter 17, so be careful banking on the promise of these government benefits.

Combining the Three Incomes

The next few chapters will explain a series of investments for generating income as we build a five-layer grid to include *Immediate Income, Middle Age Income* and *Senior Income*. A simplified example is below:

• **Immediate Income** (available now): Earning $400 per month or $4,800 per year in cash flow from a rental property.

• **Middle Age Income** (available at age 59½): Earning $333.33 per month or $4,000 per year from $100,000 in a retirement account of stocks and bonds. We are using the 4% withdrawal rule described in chapter 4.

• **Senior Income** (available at age 67): Earning $1,000 per month or $12,000 per year from Social Security.

Diversifying Income Streams

Before we move on to describing the three budgets you will need to fund for financial freedom it is worth discussing the importance of diversifying your income streams. We have already discussed that relying on the income from a job alone is very risky; if you lose your job, you lose all your income. The same lesson applies to your investment income. You don't want to put all your financial resources into a single asset class such as stocks or real estate or a single business. This is just as risky as relying solely on your job income.

During the global financial crisis, the bear market in stocks ran from October 2007 to March 2009 and the Standard & Poor's 500 stock index fell 57%. Selling stocks at the bottom of the market to pay living expenses could have crippled your plan for financial freedom. It is worth noting that the financial independence, retire early (FIRE) movement has gained significant momentum in the last decade, coinciding with a historic bull market in stocks beginning in March 2009. The FIRE trend also coincided with a strong rebound in real estate. Everyone is a brilliant investor in a bull market, it is the down markets that require real skills to properly navigate.

There will be future recessions which threaten your cash flow if you are invested solely in one asset class, particularly stocks. You must diversify your income streams to hedge against risk and add durability to your financial plan. This is why there are so many investment options in the proceeding chapters. Diversifying among a range of assets and keeping cash in an emergency fund provides you with protection in down markets.Setting up an emergency fund and managing risk are specific tasks you will work through in the *10 Stages Workbook*.

Three Budgets for Financial Freedom

Now that you understand the three categories of income, **Immediate Income**, **Middle Age Income** and **Senior Income**, we will look at using these income streams to fund your three distinct budgets which includes the **Basic Living Expenses Budget**, the **Lifestyle Expenses Budget** and the **Longevity Ex-**

penses Budget. These three budgets are like climbing successive steps towards financial freedom.

Basic Living Expenses Budget

The first budget is your *Basic Living Expenses Budget* which includes housing, utilities, food, basic transportation, health care and other necessities. Essentially the five main categories of expenses from chapter 7. *Once the income from your investments can finance this budget you have reached the first major milestone of financial freedom.* You will be able to pay all your primary bills without a day job.

You can see why such an emphasis was placed on lowering your five main expenses by 25% or more along with eliminating your credit card debt. The lower your *Basic Living Expenses Budget* the easier it is to achieve this major milestone. You can also see the importance of accurately tracking your spending from chapter 7. You don't want to assume your basic annual expenses are $25,000 when they are actually $32,000. Working from accurate data is crucial for your success. Also remember inflation will progressively increase your annual expenses so you must plan to pay for these rising costs.

Depending on your family size and the cost of living in your area, this budget might be between $20,000 to $30,000 per year. *If you pay off your mortgage you can significantly reduce your housing expenses.* Eliminating your housing expenses is the fastest way to drastically cut this budget. There are multiple tasks in the *10 Stages Workbook* to help you reduce your expenses as you formulate this budget.

When you finance your *Basic Living Expenses Budget* choose stable income streams that have lower volatility. This could include interest from bonds, rents from properties in highly desirable neighborhoods with low vacancies, interest income from high quality real estate notes, or dividends from blue chip stocks. A portion might come from annuities or possibly a pension. We will cover all of these types of investments in more detail in next few chapters. Remember this is your first milestone on your financial freedom journey. Once you can cover your basic living expenses, you have achieved a major step towards financial freedom.

Lifestyle Expenses Budget

The second budget is your *Lifestyle Expenses Budget* which includes things that are nice to have but not necessities. This includes buying new clothes, travel, extra entertainment, occasionally eating out at restaurants, replacement furniture and paying for your hobbies. If you are planning on paying for a wedding or college expenses for family members, these expenses need to be part of this budget. This budget is the actual amount you intend to live on each year. This budget is in addition to your *Basic Living Expenses Budget* and may be anywhere from $10,000 to $50,000 depending on family size and lifestyle. See the example below:

Basic Living Expenses Budget: $20,000

Lifestyle Expenses Budget: $25,000

Total Budget for the Year: **$45,000**

Once you have reached a point where your income streams cover your Lifestyle Expenses Budget, you are truly financially free. You can maintain the same quality of life without working a full-time job. The investments that fund this budget can have a bit more risk than the investments in your *Basic Living Expenses Budget,* in order to earn higher returns. There is less downside risk if you incur losses in this part of your portfolio because you can always temporarily cut back on some of your activities to reduce expenses for the year.

This budget can be covered by business income, rental properties that may face higher vacancy rates, interest from higher yielding but riskier notes, the periodic sale of shares in index funds of stocks or bonds, and the sale of individual stocks you have purchased. We will explain all these investments in detail in the coming chapters.

Longevity Expenses Budget

The third budget is the *Longevity Expenses Budget* which is to pay for expenses associated with aging and higher health care expenses. These expenses occur when you are a senior citizen and may have fewer options to remain in the workforce or the ability to make major course corrections in your financial planning. *You want to factor in saving for your Longevity Expenses Budget now, don't wait until you are older.* Remember the previous lesson that workers in their 50s have a higher chance of being forced out of their job and their salaries may not recover if this occurs. Also remember from previous chapters the benefit compounding interest has on your investments; the time to save for these expenses is now.

Any medical event that impedes your mental or physical abilities will increase your cost of living and may require personalized health care. As mentioned in chapter 7, Fidelity Investments estimates that a retiring 65-year-old *couple* will need about $285,000 to cover health care and medical expenses throughout retirement. *That means saving a minimum of $142,500 each.* Health expenses are only going to increase in the coming decades, and we all need to prepare for it.

One way to significantly lower your overall expenses is to retire to a country with a lower cost of living. There are many options for living in a place with great weather and quality health care where your savings will stretch further. Even if you live overseas for only part of the year it could be a great way to stretch your budget. Some countries even offer universal health care for citizens or permanent residents.

One benefit for those in the United States is access to the federal health insurance program Medicare for people 65 and older, individuals under 65 who have certain disabilities, and for individuals of all ages who have end-stage renal disease. Medicare provides basic health care coverage to assist with doctor visits, hospital stays, diagnostic screenings and surgeries. You will want to explore the details of Medicare coverage and factor this into your *Longevity Expenses Budget* as it should help reduce some of your health-related expenses.

Funding Your Longevity Expenses Budget

If you are not sure how to finance this budget, there are three ways explained below. The first strategy is to use a designated stock fund. You and your partner will each save $10,000 in a low-cost broad index fund of stocks, like the S&P 500. You can use the Health Savings Accounts we discussed in chapter 8 to achieve this goal. Once the account is funded, leave the funds invested until you turn age 55. Then begin converting 5% of the portfolio per year to a low-cost bond index fund. When you reach age 75 the entire portfolio will be in lower risk bonds and serve as an extra resource to cover any potential longevity expenses.

A second strategy is using a deferred annuity. At age 50 you purchase a deferred annuity that begins paying out when you turn 70 years old. At age 70 the annuity will provide monthly income to help cover any medical expenses. It can also be a way to supplement the *Senior Income* you receive from a government superannuation fund or Social Security. We will discuss annuities in detail in chapter 17.

A third strategy is to buy a rental property and pay it off over the next 15-20 years by using the rents from your tenants. When you sell this property, the proceeds will fund your *Longevity Expenses Budget*. This is my preferred approach, but all three are viable options.

One additional approach to finance this budget is to apply any inheritance you receive into one or a combination of the three options listed above. Many families are not comfortable talking about wills and future inheritances, but a frank conversation could be of tremendous value as you plan and budget for these expenses.

Simplify Investments in Your Senior Years

One other factor to consider is that in your senior years you may wish to reduce the complexity of your portfolio. Older investors may find they lack the energy to manage a wide array of complex investments. As you age consider selling some of your rental properties or shifting more sophisticated investments to ones that are easier to track such as certificates of deposit, bonds, or possibly annuities. This strategy also reduces stress, as you are less worried about exposure to market volatility.

You will be taken step-by-step through the task of creating these three budgets as you complete the *10 Stages Workbook* at www.LoadedforLife.com.

Key Takeaways:

•   You will have three types of budgets in your long-term financial plan to cover your **Basic Living Expenses**, **Lifestyle Expenses**, and **Longevity Expenses.**

•   Reducing your expenses by 25% or more and eliminating credit card debt will help you reach the milestone of covering your *Basic Living Expenses Budget* which is the first major step to financial freedom. If you can pay off your mortgage, you can also significantly reduce expenses under this budget.

•   Once you have a portfolio that provides income to cover your *Lifestyle Expenses Budget* you are truly financially free and no longer need a full-time job.

• You will need to set some money aside to fund a *Longevity Expenses Budget* to pay for your health care needs as a senior citizen. You have three strategies for funding your *Longevity Expenses Budget*, using stocks, a deferred annuity or buying a rental property. You may also consider a combination of all three, while recognizing that health care expenses are only expected to rise in the coming years and your options in the workforce may narrow as you age.

• You could consider retiring overseas to stretch your dollar further but verify available medical care and other services as part of your due diligence.

• As you think about these three budgets also think of income as falling into three categories.

• **Immediate income:** Accessible as soon as you create it with no age restrictions or tax penalties; includes income from non-tax deferred investments, and from entrepreneurial ventures such as side hustles or small businesses.

• **Middle Age Income:** Only accessible without penalty in middle age, perhaps age 59½; includes income from tax deferred retirement account investments.

• **Senior Income:** Accessible in your late 60s or early 70s and may include superannuation benefits, public pensions such as Social Security Retirement Benefits or annuities.

CHAPTER 14: INVESTMENTS

At this point you have the tools you need to track your spending, accurately calculate your actual hourly wage, and dramatically reduce your expenses by 25% or more. You also know to create three key budgets to cover your *Basic Living Expenses, Lifestyle Expenses* and *Longevity Expenses*. You will also be looking at creating different categories of income to include *Immediate Income, Middle Age Income* and *Senior Income* to fund the three budgets.

The next step is looking at various investments to generate this income and end your reliance on a full-time job. You will want to diversify income streams to hedge against risks such as rental property vacancies, stock market downturns, and the possibility of the government reducing future Social Security benefits. You also want to maintain a sustainable debt ratio so if a recession occurs you won't run out of cash and be forced to sell assets when prices are declining.

Look Ahead at the Next Few Chapters

The next two chapters will provide an introduction to investments, starting with government bonds, then stocks, rental properties, and peer to peer lending options, as well as other investments. At the end of each chapter there is a grid that shows the potential income streams from small, medium, and large sized portfolios of these investments. These investment grids are combined at the end of each chapter to show how layering your investments creates the desired diverse income streams.

Diversify for Time Commitment

Every investment requires a certain amount of time to manage with some being more time intensive than others. You want to diversify your portfolio to include some investments that are less time intensive. You don't want to trade a full-time job for a full-time job managing investments. So, look to create this time balance in your investments.

Introduction to Investments

The next two chapters are written assuming this information is new to readers, therefore parts may be a review for experienced investors. These chapters are designed to ensure readers who are new to personal finance have a clear understanding of how these investments work and their potential risks. Similarly, the follow-on chapter will cover annuities, pensions, and Social Security Retirement Benefits. There are also chapters on entrepreneurship, small businesses, and side hustles which are strategies to augment income from your investments. We will then do a deeper dive into investing in stocks and real estate as they will be key components of your financial plan.

U.S. Treasuries

U.S. Treasuries are bonds issued by the federal government to individuals and entities who loan the U.S. government money. Many investors outside of the United States own Treasuries. Treasuries are divided into three categories based on the length of their maturities. Treasury Bills have maturities of less than one year and have the lowest interest rates. Treasury Notes are medium term debt with maturities between two and ten years, usually the longer the term, the higher the interest rate.

Treasury Bonds are longer-term notes which mature in 30 years and offer a higher interest rate for this longer duration. One benefit of U.S. Treasuries for U.S. citizens is that the interest earned is exempt from taxation at the state and local level *but is subject to federal taxes*. Loaning Uncle Sam money is low risk, and a low time commitment, but provides a low return. It will require a significant amount of capital invested in Treasury Bonds, which currently yield close to 3% per year, to generate a worthwhile return. Earning $3,000 on a $100,000 investment is barely keeping up with inflation so your real return is quite low.

Inflation risk and the risk of rising interest rates, which will make existing bonds less valuable if newer bonds are issued with a higher return, are the two main dangers associated with Treasuries. Still many investors like Treasuries because they view them as being very low risk (protected from default risk) because the bonds are unconditionally backed by the full faith and credit of the U.S. government.

Some investors also purchase a series of bonds, both short-term and long-term, on a rolling basis, which is called laddering. Laddering allows investors to spread their investments among various rates of return to reduce their interest rate risk, and to provide a systematic return of their principal over time. In periods of very high inflation the yield on treasuries can rise; in 1981 one-year Treasury Bills hit interest rates of 14.54%.

State and Local Bonds

In addition to Treasuries, there are also bonds issued by state or municipal governments. Some of these bonds come with tax free interest from state income taxes. Conduct your due diligence on state and local bonds regarding risk. In 2017 after years of financial mismanagement, bonds issued by the State of Illinois were downgraded to "junk" status which is a rating that indicates the bonds are not investment grade and there is serious risk that the bond will not be repaid in full. Similarly, in 2013 the city of Detroit filed for bankruptcy and investors holding Detroit city bonds received only 74 cents for each dollar invested in the city's bonds.

Certificates of Deposit

A certificate of deposit (CD) is a savings certificate issued by a bank or credit union that provides a fixed interest rate for a specific duration of time. The duration can be as short as three months or up to several years, with the rate of return being higher the longer the duration. Like bonds, some investors prefer to ladder their CDs, which provides some interest to spend and the principal to reinvest. Current rates on a one-year CDs are just above 2% meaning the one-year return on a $100,000 would only be $2,000. *This means you are barely beating inflation, so your actual return is very low.* CDs are protected from default risk as they are insured up to $250,000 by the federal government under the Federal Deposit Insurance Corporation (FDIC).

The current low rate of return for CDs make them a poor choice for long-term investing, but they can be a relatively risk-free way to park money you need within the next year. I have invested the down payments for future real estate purchases in short-term CDs to get a better return on the money than a traditional savings account. CD rates are not always low, in periods of high inflation, interest rates on CDs will climb. In July 1984 one-year rates on CDs were above 11%.

Corporate Bonds

Corporate bonds are essentially loaning money to a business, just like Treasuries are loaning money to the federal government. The business issues a security to the investor promising to repay the bondholder their principal with interest. The interest is usually paid out twice a year. The rate of return is generally fixed and the yield depends on the credit rating of the entity (the company) issuing the bond.

For example, if Disney is performing well and is quite profitable, and has a strong credit rating it may offer bonds with a lower interest rate because investors see it as a safe investment. Disney doesn't need to offer a high rate of return to entice people to buy their bonds. As an opposite example, if a company is in financial trouble, there is a perceived risk that the company could default on the debt (credit risk). Therefore, the company will need to offer a bond with a higher yield in order to entice buyers to accept this risk. As mentioned before if the bond is seen as highly risky it will be downgraded to "junk" status, which means it is not investment grade. Essentially, this is buyer beware, but there are many investors who invest in these types of bonds.

An easier option for investing in bonds is through bond funds offered by brokerage firms like Vanguard. The bond funds have low fees and diversify holdings across many bonds to reduce risk. There are also Exchange Traded Funds (ETFs) that mirror these bond funds which allow you to invest in a broad portfolio of bonds in the same way you invest in a broad index of stocks. The benefit of any broad index for bonds or stocks is that they require a relatively low commitment of your time.

I personally like the Vanguard Total Bond Market ETF which trades under the symbol BND. This ETF is a broad portfolio of U.S. investment grade bonds designed to keep pace with U.S. bond market returns. Bonds appeal to investors seeking to secure a relatively reliable income stream over the medium or long term. As some investors grow older, bonds become more appealing due to the relatively stable rates of return and less volatility when compared to stocks.

Stocks

Buying a share of stock is essentially buying a small portion of equity in a publicly traded company, hence, why stocks are also called equities. Generally, if the company performs well and profits increase, the shares goes up in value. If the company loses money, the shares fall in value. Many companies also pay out a portion of the profits to shareholders in the form of a quarterly dividend. *However, not all stocks pay dividends.* Faster growing technology companies usually don't as they prefer to reinvest their profits into growing the business. Well known business stalwarts traditionally pay a regular dividend between 2% and 3% of the share price per year.

These dividends can be a steady stream of income for investors each quarter without having to sell any shares. Stocks can experience significant volatility which means their share prices rise and fall based on factors related to the specific company, the specific business sector, or broader economic trends. Because of this volatility stocks should be viewed as a long-term investment. *If you need the money in the next three to five years it should not be invested in stocks.*

Strategies for Investing in Stocks

The bulk of your stock portfolio should be invested consistently and systematically in a broad index of stocks instead of trying to pick individual stocks. *Many studies have proven that most stock picking professionals, let alone average investors, are not able to beat the market averages.* But people still try. I have made this mistake several times and would have been better off sticking with index funds. The average rate of return for the S&P 500, a broad index of 500 U.S. companies, has been about 10% per year from 1928 to 2014. This has not been a smooth progression, and there were some nail-biting years starting with the Great Depression of the 1930's, several recessions since, and most recently during the 2007-08 financial crisis. However, history has shown that in the long run you will see a positive trend line of returns coupled with regular payments of dividends.

Individual Shares

Despite the caveat that most people don't consistently pick winning individual stocks, most people can't help but buy individual shares for a few select companies. When you see successful companies which perform well year after year it is hard not to buy some of their shares. If you plan to buy individual stocks, try to keep these holdings to 5-10% of your total portfolio to protect against the downside risk of an individual company going out of business. Look at Enron and WorldCom as companies that were performing extremely well until they rapidly collapsed due to fraud.

Don't hold a large amount of your employer's stock. You rely on this company for your paycheck and if most of your portfolio consists of its stock you are doubling your risk. *If the company fails, you will lose both your portfolio and your paycheck.* Sell some of the shares to diversify into a broad index of stocks or other investments.

Forget Timing the Market, But Buy in a Panic

A perennial mistake of investors is trying to time the market by selling with the hope of buying back the shares at a lower price. The market is unpredictable and can make major swings in either direction within a single trading day. Avoiding the urge to tinker with your portfolio is made easier if you don't listen to the stock pros on the news trying to make daily and weekly predictions on stock movements.

When a bear market occurs, which is characterized by a 20% drop in the asset class, put more cash into stocks. This is the time to buy stocks, not sell. Remember Warren Buffet's advice; *"be greedy when others are fearful and fearful when others are greedy"*. Buying extra shares during bear markets can increase your long-term returns. Similarly, when a bear market hits, refrain from making withdrawals from your stock portfolio. Use other income streams until stocks recover; this will add years to the life of your portfolio.

Tax Loss Harvesting with Stocks

Tax loss harvesting has become increasingly popular with the emergence of robo-advisor companies. Essentially tax loss harvesting is selling one fund at a loss and then immediately buying a *similar* fund. As discussed in the chapter on taxes, capital gains losses up to $3,000 per year can be deducted against other income on your U.S. federal taxes. *You cannot immediately repurchase the same exact fund or stock within 31 days or else the IRS will disallow the loss, which is called the wash sale rule.* Otherwise investors would just sell stocks and buy them back immediately to have a nice tax deduction. Tax loss harvesting only works in non-tax deferred accounts, like a traditional brokerage account. Don't try to use it in a Roth IRA account because you are not allowed to take the losses on your taxes.

Stock Index Funds

As mentioned above, stocks can either be bought as individual shares, like a share of Microsoft or as an index fund which is a collection of shares of many companies such as all 500 companies in the Standard & Poor's index. Examples of broad index funds include Vanguard Total Stock Market Index Fund. The Admiral shares symbol is VTSAX or its exchange traded fund (ETF) equivalent is the symbol VTI. If you prefer to invest in the S&P 500 index, which includes the 500 companies in the Standard and Poor's Index, you can purchase the low fee Vanguard Admiral Shares under the symbol VFIAX or as an ETF under the symbol VOO.

By investing in a stock index fund, you are diversifying your holdings among hundreds and hundreds of companies. If you consistently contribute to this same index fund over time you are dollar cost averaging, buying when the fund is going up and down. Dollar cost averaging protects you from trying to time the market. Make sure your index fund choices are truly low cost from a reputable company like Vanguard. Other companies charge higher fees for the same service. An analysis by NerdWallet found that paying 1% in fees on an average retirement portfolio over a 40-year period could cost you $590,000.

Mixing a Portfolio of Stocks and Bonds

There are many ways to create a mixed portfolio of stocks, bonds, and other investments to diversify your holdings. A basic formula is 60% stocks and 40% bonds which you will remember from the 4% rule discussed in chapter 4. Generally, you want a relatively simple formula that is easy to maintain and that matches your appetite for risk, because you don't want to abandon your strategy during market downturns, which is a surefire way to lose money.

Shares in Private Equity Firms

The next investment we will look at is private equity shares. These are shares in a partnership that is publicly traded like stocks, but often have a higher annual yield, including some above 8% per year. These businesses usually focus on acquiring undervalued assets or businesses and then seek to extract value by splitting up the asset or implementing a plan to reduce costs and improve the performance of the business. The shares will rise or fall in value over time based on the performance of the underlying business and the broader stock market.

Examples of publicly traded private equity shares include Blackstone (symbol BX), Fortress Investment Group (FIG) and Kohlberg Kravis Roberts symbol (KKR). These firms are susceptible to risk if private money is not available to fund their acquisitions of assets or the government passes regulation that negatively affects their business model. Like stocks, the shares provide a steady stream of cash in the form of distributions instead of dividends.

Since these are shares in a partnership, at tax time you will receive a K-1 which will need to be reported on your income tax return. Although reporting this income is not difficult, you may want to check with a tax preparer or follow the prompts for a K-1 on your tax preparation software.

Master Limited Partnerships (MLPs)

MLPs are publicly traded shares in a partnership that derives cash flow from owning assets in real estate, commodities, or natural resources. The shares rise or fall in value based on the performance of the underlying assets and business. Examples are Magellan Midstream Partners LP (symbol MMP) or Enterprise Products Partners (symbol EPD). MLPs provide cash distributions to shareholders that are often above 5% per year, providing a higher yield than traditional stocks.

MLPs expose shareholders to market gyrations of the company and the underlying sector in which they are invested, such as the oil and gas sector. MLPs are like shares in private equity firms, in that you will receive a K-1 to report your income on your tax return. This is not difficult to do, but you may want to have a conversation with a tax preparer or follow the prompts for a K-1 on your tax software.

Real Estate Investment Trusts (REITs)

REITs are entities that invest in physical real estate, which allows investors to have exposure to the real estate market without owning an individual property. REITs pay the bulk of their profits to shareholders as a distribution, which can result in an annual yield of 4% to 5%. REITS are publicly traded and you can invest in specific types of real estate such as apartment buildings, senior care facilities, or shopping malls. REITS also have special tax implications, which should be reviewed with a tax preparer or on your tax preparation software.

*Annual Income from Three Sample Portfolios, **Level 1***

Please review this next section closely, as it is the first of five levels on creating a diverse investment portfolio. Adding the five levels together will build your entire portfolio. Each level shows the amount of sustainable annual income you can expect from your portfolio. *You don't have to own every type of investment in each level; you will choose based on your preferences and your goal of financial freedom*

It is important to understand that the portfolio of stocks and bonds below are not measured by a rate of return, but by the **withdrawal rate**. Your stock portfolio may increase by 8% for the year, but you will only withdraw 4% as income. As we discussed in chapter 4, a withdrawal rate of 4% is sustainable for more than 30 years. If you are retiring early, in your 40s or early 50s, you may want to use an annual withdrawal rate of 3% or 3.5% to make your wealth last.

For other investments we use the **expected annual rate of return**. For example, $3,000 invested in 1-year CDs with a 2% return = $60 per year. At the end of the year the $3,000 is reinvested in CDs for the next year. There are small, medium, and large sized portfolios to show potential income rates from various sized portfolios.

Annual Income from Three Sample Portfolios, Level 1

Asset	Small Portfolio	Medium Portfolio	Large Portfolio
Long term treasuries (*3% return*)	$3,000 = $90	$10,000 = $300	$20,000 = $600
1-year CDs (*2% return*)	$3,000 = $60	$5,000 = $100	$10,000 = $200
Corporate Bonds (4% **withdrawal rate**)	$25,000 = $1,000	$50,000 = $2,000	$100,000 = $4,000
Stocks (4% **withdrawal rate**)	$50,000 = $2,000	$100,000 = $4,000	$200,000 = $8,000
Private Equity Shares (*8% return*)	$3,000 = $240	$10,000 = $800	$20,000 = $1,600
MLPs (5% return)	$3,000 = $150	$10,000 = $500	$20,000 = $1,000
REITs (5% return)	$3,000 = $150	$10,000 = $500	$30,000 = $1,500
Annual Income (Immediate income available at any age)	**$3,690**	**$8,200**	**$16,900**
Total Invested	**$90,000**	**$195,000**	**$400,000**

Key Takeaways:

• As you create a portfolio of investments for income you will consider investments based on their risk level and their time commitment.

•   You will also consider your leverage ratio, to protect against having too much debt which can lead to losses if you must sell assets at a discount.

•   Investments will provide income streams, but the more secure investments, such as Treasuries or CDs, will have a very low return that is just above inflation. The benefit of these investments is the low chance of default. They should be a relatively small amount of your portfolio, because of the lower returns.

•   Corporate bonds can provide higher returns with a bit more risk. You can purchase bonds through an ETF which makes them easier to buy and allows you to diversify among a broad portfolio of bonds.

•   Stocks, REITs, MLPs and Private Equity shares have more volatility, but the dividends or distributions will provide a regular supply of cash distributions.

•   Don't hold a large amount of your employer's stock, if the company fails you lose your retirement portfolio and your job.

•   Don't try to time the stock market by selling but do invest additional cash during bear markets, characterized by a 20% drop in asset values. You can hold your stocks in one index fund or consider other options of adding other index funds or ETFs for U.S. stocks, international stocks, and bonds. The mix you choose will be based on your risk tolerance.

•   This is **Level 1** of building a portfolio and will be the initial foundation of investments you hold. Note that some of the assets show a rate of return, but corporate bonds and stocks are listed by withdrawal rate in keeping with the 4% rule. In the next chapter we will review other investments, many of which have a higher rate of return, including rental properties and peer to peer lending, to expand your portfolio. These investments are all *Immediate Income.*

CHAPTER 15: INVESTMENT PROPERTIES, CROWDFUNDING AND NOTES

Rental Properties

Investing in rental properties is one of the best ways to achieve your financial goals. For example, Kai buys a property for $100,000 in cash and rents it for $1,200 per month. Kai's expenses for the property are 50% of the rent collected ($600) and he has $600 left over each month as profit. This equals $7,200 per year in profit or 7.2% on his $100,000 investment. Not too shabby. There are also tax deductions and depreciation that apply to rental properties that will make Kai's return closer to 9% or 10%.

Using Leverage with Rental Properties

Now what if Kai does not have $100,000 in cash, let's look at the same deal using leverage. He buys the $100,000 property using a $20,000 down payment and finances the remaining $80,000 at 5% for a 30-year period. His monthly mortgage payment is $429 and the other expenses are still $600. In this scenario the property is generating $171 per month in cash flow or $2,052 per year which is an annual return of 10.3% on his $20,000 investment. About $100 of the mortgage payment is principal the first year and this amount will increase each successive month as he pays off the mortgage. When you add in the principal, the return on his $20,000 investment is closer to 16% per year. Once you add in tax deductions and depreciation his returns will be even higher. This example highlights the value of using debt leverage that was discussed in chapter 4. If the property were to appreciate by 3% to $103,000, this additional $3,000 would increase the return on his $20,000 investment to 31%

for the year. This is before adding in tax deductions and depreciation. *Now you know why so many millionaires built their wealth through real estate.*

Real Estate is Not Liquid

Unlike some of the other investment in the last chapter, physical real estate cannot be sold quickly and if it is, it may mean selling at a discount. There are two ways to protect your real estate investments. First, don't become over leveraged by buying more properties with borrowed money than can be serviced by the rents and your other income. *Before you buy a property ask yourself if you can cover your mortgage and tax payments if the property is vacant for several months.*

Second, real estate appreciation is wholly speculative. A real estate investment needs to stand on its own through cash flow or improving the property to force up the value. Appreciation is a great benefit, but it can't be the basis for your decision to purchase the property. A failure to heed these two simple rules was the reason so many real estate investors went bankrupt during the 2007-08 global financial crisis. Chapter 20 on real estate will cover these topics in more detail.

Crowdfunding and Peer to Peer Lending

<u>Crowdfunding Personal Loans:</u> Peer to peer lending has created the opportunity for borrowers to work with individuals instead of banks. These platforms allow investors to make investments as low as $25 in unsecured personal loans. Unsecured means there is no collateral backing the debt. The rate of return varies depending on the credit rating of the borrower. The projected return can be between 5% to over 20%. The lending platform will make some efforts to collect the debt in the event of default, but if they can't, the debt is written off as a loss. An investor can spread their risk by investing across a range of loans, for example, investing $25,000 in 1,000 loans of $25 each. Personal loans are affected by the broader economic conditions;

when the economy slows, or unemployment rises, the rate of default can climb significantly.

<u>Crowdfunding Real Estate</u>: Crowdfunding real estate platforms are very similar to the personal loans described above but these loans are backed by real estate as collateral. Real estate crowdfunding also tends to have a higher minimum investment requirement, such as $500 or more to be part of a deal. The annual rate of return can be 8%-14% or more. Some platforms allow investors to take an equity stake in properties instead of a loan. Equity investments often require a longer holding time (think two to three years instead of one year), but having equity can increase returns. But if the project fails you may lose your equity, because you are an owner in the project, not a lender.

Initially crowd funding investment platforms were restricted to accredited investors, which are high net worth individuals who are viewed as more sophisticated investors. These rules have loosened to allow more people to invest in these platforms. See the appendix for details on accredited investors.

A word of caution, if your crowdfunding platform goes out of business you may face challenges in recovering your capital. This occurred with RealtyShares, a pioneer of real estate crowdfunding, which abruptly collapsed in November 2018. It has since been bought by another firm. If this occurs it can take months and years to unwind investments and recover your money. Accordingly, it is wise to spread your investments between multiple platforms and watch for any signs of the platform's business being in trouble.

Note Investing

A note is a debt obligation that is issued to finance a project like the purchase of real estate, and are similar to the lending opportunities offered by real estate crowdfunding. Purchasing notes allows investors to act like the bank, loaning the money to buy a property and having the property as collateral. As the loan is paid back with interest over months and years the owner of the note earns a nice income stream. There are firms that specialize in note investing and investors can invest in a fund of notes or purchase a specific note for a property.

For example, a real estate note bought for $15,000 with an interest rate of 9.5% provides a return of $118.75 per month or $1,425 per year. The interest provides income to live on and you reinvest the principal in another note to perpetuate the income stream. Notes provide investors with the opportunity to invest in real estate without having to manage the property or find tenants. If notes are performing (that is they are paying on time) they are less time intensive, so you can focus your time on other investments. If the borrower stops paying on the note you may have to foreclose on the property if you can't work out a payment arrangement. If this occurs, it will become a much more time intensive investment.

Private Money

Private money is when individuals provide loans to support a business or a real estate project. With private money, the interest rate and the terms of the loan vary depending on the negotiation between the private money lender and the borrower. Private money lenders are usually familiar with the borrower's prior business or real estate experience and have seen a track record of success.

An example of a private money transaction is you loan Diane $50,000 to buy a house. Diane intends to spend $10,000 to renovate the house and sell it for $85,000. The $50,000 you lend Diane has an interest rate of 14% per year, along with a point, which is a fee equal to 1% of the loan, or $500 that is paid up front. The loan is secured against the house Diane purchased. If Diane does not repay the loan, and you two are unable to come to an agreement, such as extending the term of the loan, you would have the option of foreclosing on the house to recover your $50,000.

Alternatively, at the outset of loan negotiations you could offer to split a portion of the profits once the property is sold and offer Diane a lower interest rate. In this example, you loan Diane $50,000 to renovate the house at an interest rate of 7% but when she sells, you receive 25% of the profit from the deal. There are many ways to structure these types of deals depending on your creativity and what you are hoping to achieve with your money.

Annual Income from Three Sample Portfolios, **Level 2**

This section adds to last chapter's Level 1 grid (shaded gray) by including the investments in this chapter. We use the same format of small, medium, and large portfolios and the annual income created. You will notice that the investments in Level 2 generate a higher return than Level 1 but come with a bit more risk.

Level 2 includes both properties that still have a mortgage and properties that are paid off. Once the loan on a rental property has been paid off, the income stream will be much higher. For the sake of simplicity, this portfolio assumes that every property was purchased for $100,000. For the properties with mortgages, the down payment was $20,000. In the bottom row for Total Invested, the down payment of $20,000 for each mortgaged property and $100,000 for each paid off property is included. The assumed rental profits per month for mortgaged properties is $150 and $600 for paid off properties. The returns don't include appreciation which can be a significant contributor to your net worth. All these investments are *Immediate Income.*

Chart on next page

Annual Income from Three Sample Portfolios, **Level 2**:

Asset	Small Portfolio	Medium Portfolio	Large Portfolio
Long term treasuries (3% return)	$3,000 = $90	$10,000 = $300	$20,000 = $600
1-year CDs (2% return)	$3,000 = $60	$5,000 = $100	$10,000 = $200
Corporate Bonds (4% withdrawal rate)	$25,000 = $1,000	$50,000 = $2,000	$100,000 = $4,000
Stocks (4% withdrawal rate)	$50,000 = $2,000	$100,000 = $4,000	$200,000 = $8,000
Private Equity Shares (8% return)	$3,000 = $240	$10,000 = $800	$20,000 = $1,600
MLPs (5% return)	$3,000 = $150	$10,000 = $500	$20,000 = $1,000
REITs (5% return)	$3,000 = $150	$10,000 = $500	$30,000 = $1,500
Mortgaged Rental Property	1 home = $1,800	3 homes = $5,400	5 homes = $9,000
Paid off Rental Property	1 home = $7,200	3 homes = $21,600	5 homes = $36,000
Peer to Peer Lending (9% Return)	$5,000 = $450	$10,000 =$900	$25,000 =$2,250
Private Money Loan (14% Return)	$20,000 = $2,800	$30,000 = $4,200	$50,000 = $7,000
Notes (9.5% Return)	$15,000 = $1,425	$30,000 = $2,850	$50,000 = $4,750
Annual Income (Immediate income available at any age)	**$17,365**	**$43,150**	**$75,900**
Total Invested	**$250,000**	**$625,000**	**$1,125,000**

Key Takeaways:

• Real estate will be a key component of your investment strategy and you will use leverage to purchase properties to create cash flow. Over time as you pay these properties off, the monthly cash flow will increase.

• Crowdfunding and peer to peer lending platforms can be a way to invest in loans or in equity in real estate without having to buy a physical property. Review the prospectus of each investment very closely. If the crowdfunding platform fails, you may lose some of your capital or experience delays in repayment. To mitigate this risk, spread your investments across multiple platforms.

• Notes and private loans are a great way to invest in real estate once you have built up some capital. There is tremendous flexibility in how you structure these investments and the returns can be quite high, without the day-to-day challenges of managing real estate.

• You can now compare the lower risk, lower return investments of Level 1 to the higher return, moderate risk investments of Level 2.

• Remember that stocks and real estate will likely be your two largest holdings as they can provide returns well above inflation. This will help ensure that your income will maintain its purchasing power over time.

• Take the time to learn more about each of the investments in this chapter before you invest. As with any investment, conduct the necessary due diligence and consider possible downside risks.

• As you create a higher net worth and become an accredited investor you can increase your access to more complex investment opportunities.

CHAPTER 16: RETIREMENT ACCOUNTS

The most common retirement account is the deferred compensation plan or tax-deferred compensation plan. With these types of accounts you contribute a portion of your salary each year pre-tax for retirement. In addition, your contribution usually benefits from matching contributions from your employer or the government. These funds will eventually be taxed when you withdraw them in retirement. The investment options for these accounts can vary but most allow you to invest in a range of stocks and bonds. These accounts are a great tool for lowering your current taxes as well as helping you pay less tax on this money in retirement when you are more likely to be in a lower tax bracket.

For example, if the next $10,000 you earn in your job is taxed at 24% it will cost you $2,400 in taxes. But if you contribute the $10,000 to your retirement account and withdraw it after you quit working full-time you will be in a lower tax bracket. The $10,000 might be taxed at 10% and you only pay $1,000 in income tax. Hence, you saved $1,400.

In the United States, these tax deferred retirement accounts include the 401k, 403b, Thrift Savings Plan or other names but they all operate the same way. Other countries have similar versions such as New Zealand's KiwiSaver where participants have contributions deducted from their pay at the rate of either 3%, 4%, 6%, 8% or 10% for retirement. The account holder benefits from government and employer contributions. Australia has the Superannuation Fund, funded by employers contributing 9.5% of the employee's salary via the compulsory Superannuation Guarantee payments. Australians can add more money to their account from either before or after-tax contributions. The Australian government will also match 50 cents for every $1 of contributions in after-tax earnings up to a certain maximum per year. For more details on retirement accounts see www.LoadedforLife.com.

Middle Age Income

As we continue to think of income as falling into one of three categories *Immediate Income, Middle Age Income* and *Senior Income,* the withdrawals from retirement accounts are a vital part of your *Middle Age Income.* You will begin accessing these funds between the ages of 55-67, depending on when you become eligible to make withdrawals. People usually begin withdrawals as they transition out of full-time employment or when they face major expenses such as paying for a child's college education, for a wedding, or caring for elderly parents. These tax deferred retirement accounts have a few benefits that make them a great way to save for retirement.

Matches Are Free Money

I want to delve a little deeper into the benefits of these accounts that were mentioned in the first paragrahp of the chapter. The first benefit is the employer or government match. If you contribute an amount that ensures the full match you are receiving a 100% return on your contribution. If your employer matches your $5,000 contribution, you have now saved $10,000 for retirement and doubled your money with zero risk. There are very few opportunities to double your investment with zero risk. *At a minimum contribute enough to your account to get the full employer match.*

The second benefit is deferring the taxes which was mentioned at the start of the chapter. Almost all of us will be in a higher tax bracket while working compared to when we retire or switch to part-time work. By using a tax deferred retirement account, you get to save the difference of these brackets. As we saw if you contribute $10,000 to your account while working full-time to avoid a 24% tax bracket and then withdraw the money in retirement when it is taxed at 10% you save $1,400. Over your entire career of deferring income to retirement accounts, you will save tens of thousands of dollars in taxes.

Impact of Compounding

The third benefit of these retirement accounts is compounding interest. If Simone contributes $14,000 to her account with an employer match of $5,000. Simone is now saving $19,000 per year and the $5,000 match is free money. If Simone is 25 years old and contributes $19,000 to her account for ten years, she would have $190,000 saved for retirement. Not bad, but it gets better! If Simone invests her contributions biweekly in a mix of stocks and bonds that grow at a conservative annual rate of 7% for these ten years, her account will be approximately $275,000. If Simone never contributes another dollar but maintains a 7% average annual return for the next 20 years, her account will be over $1 million at the age of 55. *Simone is a millionaire from this one decision of saving for ten years and then not touching the money for the following 20 years.*

There will be volatility in the stock market from year to year, but historically a fund that tracks the S&P 500 index will earn a 10% average annual return (1928 to 2014). Simone only used a return of 7% per year, which factors in the potential for some significant downside risk in her future returns. If you wish to experiment in calculating potential returns on different investment amounts, please see the investment calculator at www.SmartAssets.com.

Incentivizing Saving

You might be wondering why the government allows people who save in retirement accounts to pay less tax. The government is using the tax code to incentivize behavior that it sees as valuable. The government recognizes that Social Security Retirement Benefits are not enough for an adequate retirement, so they are using the tax code to induce both individuals and their employers to encourage saving for retirement. This is a great opportunity and by taking advantage of it, you can accelerate your progress towards financial freedom.

Early Withdrawal Penalties

To discourage people from withdrawing the money from these accounts prior to retirement age, the government may impose a penalty on early withdrawals in addition to having to pay regular income taxes on the money. In the United States, the early penalty is 10% of the funds withdrawn plus income taxes if the account holder is younger than 59½ years old. However, there are several ways around these penalties to access the funds before age 59½, which are included in a grid in Appendix 2 and on LoadedforLife.com.

Some countries have options to make a penalty-free early withdrawal if you become seriously ill and need to pay for treatment or if you are buying your first property. Contributing to these accounts and using the employer match is a clever way to accelerate saving for the deposit on your first property. Essentially using your retirement plan to also advance your real estate goals.

Caveats for Early Retirees

People looking to retire very early, 30s or 40s, should be careful not to allocate too much to these retirement accounts. These funds are *Middle Age Income* and will not be accessible until you are in the age range of 55-67. For very early retirees it is preferable to invest more heavily in investments that provide *Immediate Income*. But, you will miss out on the employer/government match and the deferred tax benefits. This is something to think about as you review and modify your long-term plan.

It is also worth mentioning that you can't keep funds in your account indefinitely. Many accounts make account holders to take required minimum distributions (RMDs) when they reach a certain age. In the United States it is age 72 although there are proposals to raise this to age 75. The RMD is a way for the government to ensure they recover taxes on these funds and to prevent account owners from passing all these funds untaxed to their heirs.

Exercise Some Caution on Withdrawals

As discussed in chapter 4 under the 4% rule, exercise caution in tapping these funds if a major recession occurs in the first five years of retirement. It is better to return to work, at least part time, to allow your account balances to recover. It is also wise to use an annual withdrawal rate below 4% per year if have small account balance. An annual withdrawal rate of 3% or 3.5% will extend the life of your portfolio for years.

Other Benefits of Retirement Accounts

There are two additional benefits of retirement accounts to assist you in building wealth. The first is as proof of reserves when qualifying for a mortgage. A bank will want to see that you have a sufficient amount of assets in reserve that can be liquidated to pay back the loan. A retirement account can be those reserves. Personally, our retirement accounts regularly helped us to secure mortgages, particularly after the global financial crisis when lenders became skittish about lending on real estate.

The second benefit is that many deferred compensation plans allow employees to take loans against their balance, which they pay back over a few years through salary deductions. If they don't pay back the loan, the outstanding balance is treated as an early withdrawal and subject to taxes plus any penalties, assuming the employee is younger than the minimum retirement age. *These loans should never be taken to purchase items like cars, boats, or vacations.* They are only for the purpose of buying assets.

Roth Retirement Accounts

For workers in the United States it is also worth mentioning the Roth Individual Retirement Account (Roth IRA). The Roth IRA has become so popular I could see other countries replicating it in the future. A Roth IRA is unique because you fund the account with *after-tax* money, so it will not lower your current taxes, but the contributions, *along with any investment returns*, are tax free when withdrawn. Roth IRA accounts are a great way to build a portfolio of tax-free money. You can usually have a Roth IRA and a deferred compensation account at the same time. Once you retire you can withdraw from each of these accounts to create an income stream that includes both taxable and non-taxed income.

For example, Elvis has saved $100,000 in his Roth IRA and $400,000 in his tax deferred retirement account. Elvis intends to use the 4% rule withdrawal rate in retirement. Where Elvis lives, income below $16,000 is not taxed. In his first year of retirement Elvis withdraws $4,000 from his Roth IRA and $16,000 from his tax deferred retirement account. He will pay $0 income tax on the $16,000 because it is below the first tax bracket. He will also pay $0 tax on the $4,000 from his Roth IRA because these withdrawals are tax free. Elvis is cleverly mixing his withdrawals to reduce his taxes.

Small Business Retirement Accounts

If you have a small business in the United States, you can investigate the retirement savings options of a Solo401(k) or Simplified Employee Pension Individual Retirement Arrangement (SEP IRA) plan. These accounts create the ability to allocate a significant amount of income into tax deferred accounts. It is just one more reason why creating a small business can be an excellent way to reduce your taxes, increase your income, and defer some of this income into a tax deferred retirement account. The SEP IRA and Solo401(k) accounts require far more explanation than can be covered in this chapter but there are details about these accounts on the website LoadedforLife.com.

Annual Income from Three Sample Portfolios, **Level 3**

In this section, the *Immediate Income* investment options from Level 1 and 2 (shaded in gray) are combined with the *Middle Age Income* of Level 3. Our Level 3 income is from a tax deferred retirement account like a 401(k). Like the two previous levels, Level 3 shows three sized portfolios and the expected annual income they will provide. Remember with these retirement accounts we are not tracking the annual rate of return which will fluctuate year to year, we are using a 4% withdrawal rate each year. We expect the account to be sustainable for 30+ years at this rate.

<u>Annual Income from Three Sample Portfolios, **Level 3**</u>:

Small Portfolio   **Medium Portfolio**   **Large Portfolio**

Immediate Income from Levels 1 and 2 combined.

$17,365 $43,150 $75,900

Middle Age Income Starting Age 55-67 (Level 3)
60% Stocks/40% Bonds and 4% annual withdrawal rate.
*$100,000 = **$4,000** $300,000 = **$12,000** $600,000 = **$24,000***

Total Annual Income from Levels, 1, 2, 3 combined
$21,365 $55,150 $99,900

Key Takeaways:

• Sign up for your employer's tax deferred retirement plan and choose the option that is the closest to a broad index of stocks. If you are uneasy with volatility, you can select a fund that is a mix of stocks (60%) and bonds (40%) to diversify your holdings.

• At a minimum, contribute enough to your plan to receive the full match from your employer. This is a 100% return on your money with no risk. You will also benefit by lowering your income taxes on the amount you contribute to the plan.

• Remember the example of Simone, you can become a millionaire just from a decade of aggressive saving in your retirement account and letting the account grow over time through compounding interest.

• Tax deferred retirement accounts create an income stream that pays out in your mid-50s to mid-60s depending on your plan and will be a key component of your *Middle Age Income*.

• If you retire very early, recognize the risks of withdrawing too much of your money too quickly or having to go back to work if you experience a major down market in your first five years of retirement.

• Depending on your income level and where you live you may also be able to add a Roth IRA. If you withdraw income from a Roth IRA, it is not taxed and can be mixed with withdrawals from tax deferred plans to reduce your overall tax liability.

• If you have a small business, you can investigate the retirement savings options of a Solo401(k) or SEP IRA plan.

• Part of your long-term financial plan is to educate yourself on all the retirement account options that exist where you live and through your employer. Make it a priority to learn about these accounts now so you can benefit from them right away.

CHAPTER 17: ANNUITIES, PENSIONS AND SOCIAL SECURITY

This chapter looks at options for *Senior Income* when you reach your mid-60s or 70s. *Senior Income* may include annuities, pensions, or government superannuation like Social Security Retirement Benefits. You may not have all these income streams, but having just one can be valuable for your future finances. Don't expect Social Security Retirement Benefits to cover all your living expenses. This is a common mistake as people overestimate the amount these programs provide when they become senior citizens.

In addition, if you have not already done so, you are ready to begin Stage 2 of your 10 Stages Workbook. Stage 2 includes your next seven tasks. The workbook is your roadmap to financial independence and will move you from reading about financial freedom to making it happen. If you need a reminder of your motivations, review your reasons for starting this journey at the start of your workbook.

Annuities

Annuities are a financial product purchased from financial institutions and insurance companies to provide a fixed set of monthly income payments. Annuities can be a form of *Immediate Income* if you purchase an immediate annuity that initiates payments right away. The other option is a deferred annuity, which works more like *Middle Age Income* or *Senior Income*. The deferred annuity is purchased now, but payments don't begin until a designated future date. By delaying the payout your monthly payments are higher. For example, buying an immediate annuity for $100,000 might provide you with $425 per month in payments. But buying a $100,000 deferred annuity paying out in ten years might offer payments of $650 per month. The payment amount depends on your age and gender and your estimated life expectancy.

Investors that purchase annuities are seeking simplicity and stability; they want to insulate themselves from market volatility with guaranteed income for life. Annuities can also be bought that are indexed for inflation; they cost more, but the payments increase annually to protect against inflation eroding the purchasing power of your payments. The downside of annuities is that there are significant upfront fees and once the payments begin, it can be very expensive or impossible to make changes.

To protect against the risk of an annuitant dying before or soon after payments begin, there are options to purchase an annuity with a minimum number of payments, such as ten years of guaranteed payments. The annuitant's heirs will inherit any remaining payments. A basic immediate annuity, not indexed for inflation, might cost $100,000 and provide $425 per month or $5,100 per year in income. This is equivalent to an annual return of 5.1% on the $100,000. *However, keep in mind that you surrender the $100,000 and it will not be returned at a future date.*

Annuity for Part of Basic Living Expenses Budget

Annuities are not always a preferred investment because of their high fees and because other investments can provide more favorable returns. However, there are two scenarios where annuities might make sense. The first is using an annuity to pay for part of your *Basic Living Expenses Budget* discussed in chapter 13. If you are not retiring for several years you could purchase a deferred annuity to begin payments the year you intend to retire. For example, if your annual *Basic Living Expenses Budget* is $24,000 you could purchase an annuity that covers $12,000 (one-half) of this budget. This strategy appeals to those who are more risk averse and are looking for peace of mind. If there are market downturns, you know that half of your basic living expenses are covered.

Revisiting Deferred Annuity Strategy

The second potential scenario for an annuity is the deferred annuity for your *Longevity Expenses Budget* described in chapter 13. At the age of 50 (or before) purchase a deferred annuity that pays out when you turn 70 years old. The annuity will be less expensive because the payments don't begin for 20+ years. Purchasing this deferred annuity for $100,000 at age 50 could provide monthly payments of $1,400 starting at age 70. These annuity payments help insure you don't outlive your money and provide additional resources to pay for medical expenses.

Pensions

Although they are increasingly less common, employer pensions are a tremendous source of income for retired workers. Pension plans fall into one of two categories. The first is a defined-benefit plan in which an employer provides an employee with a monthly payment upon retirement based on the employee's earnings history and length of service.

Defined benefit plans were the norm for most employees until the 1980s when employers saw them as being too expensive. Retired workers were living longer and drawing benefits for more years, driving up the cost of offering these plans. To help reduce pension costs, employers limited or stopped offering defined benefit plans to new hires. They are increasingly rare in the private sector with only 6% of Fortune 500 employers retaining the same defined benefit plan structure from 1998 to 2017.

The U.S. federal government and some state governments still provide a defined pension plan, but these are increasingly requiring higher contributions by the employee. Congress has repeatedly suggested cutting pensions for federal employees as have state legislatures for state employees. If you retire on a pension, there is no guarantee that you will retain the same level of benefits through retirement. Fortunately, some countries have government insurance programs to try to protect pension payments but there is always a risk benefits might be reduced.

As employers moved away from defined benefit pension plans, they switch to defined-contribution plans which are the tax deferred retirement plans like a 401(k) described in the last chapter. These are not truly a pension since they are more of a retirement savings vehicle. The main advantage of defined contribution plans is that the employee owns the account and it is not something an employer can take away after retirement. But these plans don't provide a guaranteed monthly payment like a defined benefit pension. The benefits are based on the amount an individual saves in the account. Hence, you only benefit if you participate in your employer's plan and use it to your advantage.

Social Security Retirement Benefits

It is worth spending some time to explain U.S. Social Security Retirement Benefits, as it appears to be a subject of increasing unease for many future retirees. If you are not a U.S. citizen but lived and worked in the United States for more than ten years and paid into the program, you may be eligible for Social Security Retirement Benefits. Many future beneficiaries have not calculated their estimated benefits and some retirees are unfortunately expecting a significantly higher check than they will receive. *This mistaken overreliance on Social Security is one of the reasons people don't save more aggressively for retirement.*

Your Monthly Benefit

The average monthly U.S. Social Security retirement check for 2020 is $1,503 or approximately $18,036 for the year. Does this figure come as a surprise? It is important to calculate your estimated benefits now, so you know what you might receive when you begin drawing your benefits. Some recipients receive less than this amount because they worked for fewer years or had a lower salary while employed. The highest level of benefits at Full Retirement Age for 2020 is $3,011 per month or $36,132 per year. This amount is for those who had a higher salary and worked for *at least 35 years* in traditional full-time paid employment. Social Security Retirement Benefits are not tax-free, the government may tax 85% of your benefits, depending on the amount of additional income you have when you are receiving your benefits.

Not Everyone Qualifies

Not everyone who has worked in the United States qualifies for benefits; a worker must earn 40 work credits (ten years) throughout their working lifetime and pay into the system to be eligible. To be eligible for a credit in 2019 a worker must have earned at least $1,360 during the quarter. The Social Security Administration computes the actual benefit amount based on the highest income you earned during 35 years of work in which you earned credits. *Some people reading this book intend to retire early and don't intend to work for 35 years, which means their Social Security benefits will be lower and they need to factor lower benefits into their planning.* If you access your account on the Social Security Administration website, you can review details of your work history, the number of credits you have earned and see an estimate of your future monthly benefits. The Social Security Administration also provides a calculator to estimate your future benefit payments.

Full Retirement Age

You become eligible for your full Social Security Retirement Benefit when you reach your Full Retirement Age (FRA) currently 67 years old for anyone born after 1959. You can receive retirement benefits as early as age 62 but *taking benefits early reduces **all** future benefit payments*. You may also delay taking benefits until you are 70 years old, which will increase your benefits by 8% for each year you delay after your FRA. For example, if you wait until age 69.5 to start benefits you would see a 20% higher monthly payment and if you wait until age 70 your payments will be 24% higher. If you rely more heavily on your *Middle Age Income* discussed in the previous chapter from age 67 to 70 you can delay taking Social Security benefits and increase your monthly benefit by 8% for each year you delay.

Funding Social Security

The Social Security Administration funds retirement benefits in three ways. The first is a 12.4% payroll tax on earned income up to $137,700. Every worker who receives a traditional paycheck has these payroll taxes deducted (part is paid by the employee and part is paid by the employer). If your salary is above $137,700 in 2020, you will notice your take home pay increases in the latter part of the calendar year because there is no payroll tax on your salary above $137,700. The second way of funding Social Security benefits is by taxing a portion of your benefits. As mentioned before, Social Security may tax up to 85% of your benefits. The third way of funding Social Security is the interest income earned on Social Security's asset reserves, which are unfortunately steadily declining.

Social Security's Financial Troubles

According to forecasts, the Social Security Administration will pay out more in retirement benefits than it collects in revenue in 2022. The funding gap will worsen from an $18.2 billion shortfall in 2022 to a $143.8 billion shortfall in 2026. Social Security has some additional funds from the taxes it collects on benefits, but these trust funds run out in 2034. *Yes, Social Security estimates it will not be able to pay out full benefits by 2034.* Let that sink in for a minute as you consider how this may impact your expected *Senior Income*.

There are two main factors contributing to the Social Security funding gap. First, people are living longer and therefore drawing benefits for a longer number of years than originally anticipated. The government designed the program to provide benefits for the last few years of a recipient's life. However, as people live longer, they receive payments for more years and the system faces greater strain.

The second factor causing the funding gap is that there are fewer workers paying into the system as a large segment of our population retires. Fewer taxes to support the program means it is unsustainable. Social Security is facing this current crisis primarily because legislators did not responsibly raise the retirement age in line with rising life expectancy rates. Since 1960, the average life expectancy has increased from 67 years old to 76 years for men and 81 years old for women. The government designed the program properly but Congress did not manage it responsibly. It is worth noting that members of Congress who should be doing a better job of protecting this program are eligible for a special pension equal to 80% of their final salary, so personally they are less worried about needing to rely on Social Security for themselves. Think about that next time you vote.

Options for Saving Social Security

A report by the Board of Trustees that performs oversite of Social Security Retirement Benefits has suggested that by 2034 benefits need to be reduced by 23% percent or payroll taxes need to be increased somewhere between 4% and 16.5%. Another potential option is to apply payroll taxes to all income above the current $137,700 cap. And a fourth option is to raise the retirement age a few years to match current life expectancy rates. A proper solution will likely require a combination of all four of these options to reform the program and make it sustainable. Therefore, expect a future reduction in benefits, a higher retirement age and the possibility of paying higher payroll taxes.

What This Means for You

You should factor in a future reduction in Social Security Retirement Benefits into your retirement plans. *At a minimum, plan for benefits to be reduced by 15% meaning you will receive only 85% of current projected benefits. And add two years to your Full Retirement Age, hence think 69 years old not 67 years old before you can take your full benefits.* If you plan for this now you will be ready in the future and the changes will not come as a surprise or hurt your plans for financial freedom.

*Annual Income from Three Sample Portfolios, **Level 4***

In this section, the *Immediate Income* from Level 1 and 2 and the *Middle Age Income* of Level 3 (all shaded in gray) are combined with Level 4's *Senior Income*. *Senior Income* includes Social Security Retirement Benefits at Full Retirement Age (FRA) and any annuities or pensions. We use the average annual Social Security Retirement Benefits for 2019 of $17,520 with a 15% reduction of benefits to reflect a reduction in future benefits. The age for full retirement benefits is listed as 69 years old instead of the current 67, anticipating it will rise.

Social Security Retirement Benefits at FRA = $17,520

15% reduction in case benefits are reduced = -$2,628

Social Security Retirement Benefit (less 15%) = $14,892

Annual Income from Three Sample Portfolios (**Level 4**):

Small Portfolio	Medium Portfolio	Large Portfolio
Immediate Annual Income from Levels 1 and 2 combined		
$17,365	$43,150	$75,900
Middle Age Income (Level 3 Income) Age 55-67		
Tax Deferred Retirement Account from 60% Stocks / 40% Bond Mix and a 4% annual withdrawal rate.		
$100,000 = $4,000	*$300,000 = $12,000*	*$600,000 = $24,000*

Senior Income at Full Retirement Age (*Level 4 Income*) **Age 69**
Average Social Security Benefits after 15% reduction is $14,892

Total Annual Income from Levels 1,2,3 and 4 combined.

$36,257	$70,042	$114,792

Key Takeaways:

• This chapter looked at sources of *Senior Income* for your late 60s or 70s. This may include government superannuation or public pensions for senior citizens including Social Security Retirement Benefits. *Senior Income* may also include employer pensions or immediate or deferred annuities.

• Defined benefit pensions are disappearing as employers replace them with defined contribution plans like 401ks.

• The simplicity and stability of annuities may make them a desirable investment in your senior years. You can choose annuity payments indexed for inflation or not. The purchasing power of an annuity payments not indexed for inflation will decline over time.

• Annuities often have a lower rate of return compared to other investments and you surrender your principal upon purchase. The payments also end upon the death of the annuitant, unless you purchase an annuity with guaranteed payments for a minimum number of years.

• An annuity can be a way to cover a portion of your basic living expenses if you prefer that peace of mind and a deferred annuity can cover longevity expenses, purchased decades before payments begin, providing an income boost later in life.

• Social Security Retirement Benefits will provide some *Senior Income* in your sixties but the program as it currently stands is financially unsustainable. As you plan for financial freedom expect lower benefits for future generations and a higher minimum retirement age.

• You can use your *Middle Income* discussed in the previous chapter to live on to delay taking Social Security Retirement Benefits in order to increase your monthly benefit payment.

• Access your Social Security account to estimate your projected benefits but factor in an estimated reduction in benefits and a raising of the retirement age in the future. If you live in a country with a government superannuation plan for senior citizens, learn about your program and determine your future benefits.

CHAPTER 18: ENTREPRENEURSHIP AND SMALL BUSINESSES

In this chapter and the next, we delve into entrepreneurship, considerations for starting a small business, and using side hustles to create income. This is part of the process of shifting your mindset away from relying on traditional full-time employment. We will discuss the importance of using systems in your business to improve efficiency. The chapters also cover using revenue for growth to reduce your reliance on debt. Entrepreneurship can be something you pursue alone or with partners to help spread the risk or bring in skills to compliment your own. The revenue from small businesses or side hustles will be another form of *Immediate Income* and at the end of chapter 19 small business income and side hustles are factored in as Level 5 of the income grid. As you make your way through the *10 Stages Workbook*, you will also see that there are specific tasks related to entrepreneurial activities and earning some of this income.

Entrepreneurship

During my teens I had the benefit of starting two small businesses with my dad and my brother. This was a fantastic education in both the startup process and in growing a business on a lean budget. The first business was a film processing and video rental store, yep way back when movies were on VHS tapes and long before digital cameras. I worked the counter renting movies and developing film. Retail, without a supporting web sales presence, is time intensive. You only make money when you are open and the hours can be long. Some parts of the day are busy and therefore profitable, but others are slow. Each day may feel the same and some owners feel tied to the physical location of the store.

For many small retail businesses owners, it is difficult to get away for vacations unless you can systematize the business and hire a manager to run daily operations. But many small businesses don't make it to this stage for a variety of reasons. Sometimes owners can't release control of daily operations by trusting their employees or think the business can't run without their daily presence. Sometimes owners lack the vision to scale or the willingness to take the risks necessary to grow.

Learning to Pivot

Small retail businesses also face significant risks from larger, well-financed competitors. In our case, it was from Blockbuster and Hollywood Video. When these superstores emerged, it was clear our business model would not survive. We recognized and accepted that the market had fundamentally changed. Our business model was obsolete and we needed to pivot. Blockbuster Video would later become obsolete against Netflix's subscription service and the invention of streaming videos.

Currently, many retail businesses are finding they can't compete with the online shopping platforms like Amazon and must revise their business model or close. When we saw the video superstores emerge we knew it was time for a different business so we launched a small commercial sign company. We knew nothing about the sign business, but business skills are transferable. We also had very little capital to start, but we bootstrapped our way by learning from competitors, talking to customers and offering competitive pricing to secure initial sales and build a client base.

Work You Enjoy

For us, the sign business was a tremendous improvement over the video store. I preferred working outside installing signs and constantly being on the move instead of standing behind a counter. The sign business also offered various ways to hustle to increase sales and various revenue streams through repairs and new installations. We were also able to hire a few friends which made the work even more enjoyable. As we put in the effort it led to more sales and the business grew, and many days it did not feel like work, which is the ultimate goal.

As a new entrepreneur, you need to ensure your business matches your personality and the work you enjoy. If you want your weekend nights to yourself, don't open a pizza delivery business. If you don't want to get up early, don't start a bakery. If you don't want to manage a large staff that frequently turns over don't buy a major fast food franchise. This may seem obvious, but people sometimes forget to think through the day-to-day operations of what their new business will require. The idea of the business may sound much more exciting than the reality. To help prevent investing in the wrong business it is best to experiment with a job in a similar business first. I thought it would be great to own a restaurant until I waited tables for three years and saw how much work goes into running a restaurant. By working in a business, you will quickly learn what you like and don't like about the industry before you invest.

You also need to identify your strengths and weaknesses. You can't set up a single person consultancy if you don't like to sell your services or perform the record keeping and invoicing. You need to bring in staff or partners to strengthen theses areas of weakness if you want your business to be successful. It helps to get honest feedback from former co-workers or partners as we often underestimate our shortcomings. Think through all these aspects of the business before you start so you are not blindsided. Your eventual goal is to have employees running the day to day operations of the business, but before you reach that point you will be spending a significant amount of time working in the business to make it profitable and to establish the necessary systems. But take the necessary time at the front end to choose the right type of business.

Entrepreneurship as a Second Career

Although we often see images of successful start-ups launched by people in their twenties, the reality is quite different. A study by the National Bureau of Economic Research found the average age of founders of the *fastest growing* companies in the United States is 45 years old. The study also found these entrepreneurs have more experience and existing networks in the industry, which increases their likelihood of success. These factors make entrepreneurship a great option for a second career in life.

The conventional wisdom is to take the financial risks of launching a startup when you are young, have few responsibilities, and can live on less money. Having experienced the amount of work and stress required to start and grow small businesses, I take a contrarian view. My wife and I wanted to travel extensively when we were younger, and we did not want to be working 80+ hours a week in a startup. There is certainly a chance of missing out on a major success early in life, but we preferred to grow a business while still earning a salary and having more time for the things we enjoy. We found this approach reduces both risk and stress as we can learn along the way and recover from mistakes by having income from our jobs.

Create Systems from the Beginning

If you want to be an entrepreneur, you must treat your new endeavor like a proper business from day one. When we started managing rental properties, we created a professional lease (reviewed by a real estate attorney) and developed a process to take prospective tenants from the initial call, to completing the application and background checks, to signing the lease and transferring the keys. Every step of the process must be done the same way each time to ensure both fairness and the same level of professional service.

A great resource on the subject of systemizing your business is the book <u>The E-Myth Revisited</u> by Michael Gerber and there is a helpful animated introduction to his concepts on YouTube. As <u>The E-Myth Revisited</u> points out, many businesses fail because the people that start them are technicians, such as an electrician or a graphic artist. Having the skills to design great signs does not mean you have the skills to run a successful sign business. In business you must think and act like an entrepreneur, which requires creating a clear system for your employees to follow as you focus on the broader issues of growing and scaling the business. Systematization ensures that customers receive the same high-quality experience every time they use your services. These are the principles that define most brand name franchise businesses like McDonald's or Subway and is why they have been able to expand globally.

Formalizing Your Businesses

The definition of a small business can be very broad, but formalizing your business is what separates it from hobbies or side hustles. Formalizing your business means keeping proper business records, having clearly defined written steps to follow for each aspect of the business. You also want to open a business bank account separate from your personal accounts. The business may also be set up as a distinct legal entity such as limited liability company (LLC) which means filing a separate business tax return from a personal tax return. These are all steps to consider right from the beginning of starting your business. It is more difficult to try to go back and reinstitute these systems after your business has grown. These systems are the foundation to ensure your business grows properly from the start. Establishing these systems requires spending the money to get professional advice to avoid common mistakes, but don't try to skip these steps to save startup capital. This is where you should be spending your money.

Creating Time Flexibility

One of the best elements of small businesses, if structured and systemized properly, is its ability to provide flexibility with your time. Traditional day jobs usually require being physically present for a set number of hours each day; you get paid for showing up and working each day. As we discussed earlier this is a process of trading your time for money. With a business, you can move away from specifically trading your time for money. Properly structuring a business and its operations means it can generate enough revenue to pay staff which frees up your time for other more productive pursuits.

Working with the right partners can be a key for this type of success. For example, when we lived in Washington D.C., we heard about two brothers who opened a bar to finance their respective snowboarding and surfing passions. One brother managed the bar for six months while the other brother pursued his sport. The arrangement allowed each of the brothers to work half the year while still having year-around income. For these partnerships to succeed you need to work with trustworthy people and have a clearly defined rules and responsibilities. You can't rush creating flexibility; it takes time to bring a business to the point where it can operate successfully under the management of employees. If you design and execute properly, your plan will help to create a business that can generate returns while still providing you the flexibility to pursue other interests.

Revenue Drives Growth

A key to hedging risk in small businesses is to cap the amount of startup capital invested. Sinking more and more money into a fledgling business can put a broader financial freedom plan in jeopardy. To reduce risk, your startup capital should be cash reserves or from a manageable amount of debt. If the business fails, you need to be able to repay the debt either by returning to full-time work or from your other income streams. This initial injection of funds is to launch quickly and to serve as working capital, but once the business is operating only revenue can drive future growth.

In the book <u>Millionaire Real Estate Agent</u>, Gary Keller, the co-founder of Keller Williams Real Estate, recommends that businesses should *lead with revenue.* He suggests that a business that spends revenue instead of relying on debt can operate indefinitely. This may be a slower path to growth, but it is a sustainable way to grow. The business expands as the cash flow allows for expansion. Even when business improves, the owner must have the discipline to prevent expenses from jumping ahead of revenue.

Expanding too quickly and letting costs rise is frequently why businesses failure. When we first started our real estate business, we used this ethos. We chose to acquire fewer properties, pay them off quicker and use the cash flow to service the next purchase. Our business model minimizes risk because we are not highly leveraged, and we can cover the mortgages in the event of an economic downturn. If we have an extended vacancy at a property or two, we can rely on the rents from the other properties to cover all expenses and still pay ourselves. We would have definitely become wealthier if we were more aggressive, but we chose to avoid becoming highly leveraged and possibly losing some properties in a recession. We subscribe to the belief that we would rather not have something new, than to see something we worked for taken away.

Beware of Personal Guarantees

Your efforts to reduce risks should include trying to avoid signing personal guarantees for business-related activity. A personal guarantee is a legal contract that means a lender can pursue your personal assets, like your home, if you default on business debt. Sometimes a personal guarantee is unavoidable to get financing but make sure the amount of debt is manageable and try to structure the agreement where your personal guarantee diminishes each year until it is gone. For example, you could negotiate a 100% personal guarantee in year one, but an 80% personal guarantee in year two, followed by 60% in year three and onward until it is eliminated.

Also, make sure everyone in the deal signs the personal guarantee at the same time. One of my friends was in a real estate project with three other partners and all four were to sign personal guarantees. Everything was going fine with the deal until the global financial crisis set in and the project began to fail. At this point, when he met with the lenders, he learned that the other investors never signed a personal guarantee. In the fallout from the global financial crisis many banks discovered they did not properly document real estate loans or that they had made glaring mistakes like overlooking signatures on key documents. Fortunately, the lenders did not enforce the personal guarantee against my friend, but he learned a valuable lesson of making sure that all partners are present in the room to sign at the same time.

Treasure Trove of Tax Deductions

Entrepreneurs usually focus on the profit side of launching a business, but owning or being a partner in a small business opens the door to numerous tax deductions. As I have mentioned before, learning about taxes is one of the keys to wealth creation. There can be tax deductions for using part of your home as an office, deducting business related vehicle costs, as well as deducting expenses for internet services, computers, software, printers, and mobile phones related to your business operations. One of the resources I used to understand business tax deductions, as well as for real estate, were the books offered by Nolo.com.

Investing in Start-Ups

Some investors think its better to invest in other entrepreneurs instead of starting their own business. This strategy can work particularly with proven business models, but be cautions when it comes to investing in innovative start-ups. Similar to the fallacy of twentysomethings being the most successful entrepreneurs, there is a similar myth around people becoming massively wealthy by investing in early stage start-ups.

The idea of venture capital sounds much more exciting and successful than it really is. For every standout success like Amazon, PayPal or Google, there are thousands and thousands of failures. The vast majority of early stage companies fail, with only 20% of these businesses even proving profitable. This means they only make a profit, it does not mean they reward their investors with a reasonable return on their money. As these are equity investments, if the business fails, you lose your investment. In addition, these types of investments usually require committing your capital for multiple years and it is difficult to get your money back any earlier. We have some experience investing in start-ups and there is an article on LoadedforLife.com entitled Investing in Startups: Six Factors to Know. Be cautious when it comes to start-ups, it usually requires investing in dozens of companies hoping that one is a major success.

Key Takeaways:

•   If you are interested in starting a small business, take the time to explore several types of businesses to find one that matches your personality. Experiment by taking a job in the business to understand the industry and its daily operations.

•   Keep an eye on larger business trends to see if a new major competitor means your business has become obsolete; if so, it is time to pivot.

• Success often depends on your ability to systematize your business, allowing it to grow and provide consistent high-quality service to your customers. Businesses can provide income and flexibility of time when managed correctly, which may require bringing in the right partners.

• Lead with revenue to grow in a way that reduces the chance of failure or incurring significant debt.

• Be wary of personal guarantees that put your personal assets at risk if your business fails.

• Small businesses open the door to numerous tax advantages that will help facilitate your wealth creation.

• Investing in start-ups often sounds more exciting and profitable than it really is and there are several key factors on LoadedforLife.com to consider before investing in start-ups.

CHAPTER 19: SIDE HUSTLES

I appreciate society's current enthusiasm with the side hustle/gig economy, but it is important to filter out some of this hype. Side hustles can supplement your income and may grow into a legitimate small business, but the income is rarely enough to justify quitting a full-time job. One study found that the number of jobs in the gig economy (with companies like Uber, Lyft, Etsy, Airbnb, and TaskRabbit) are actually relatively small, representing only 0.5% of all jobs. This number is remaining steady, likely due to the high turnover rates of people working these side hustles. Essentially, one new person starts driving for Uber while another quits.

Still Trading Time for Money

When Uber first started in 2009 there were claims that drivers were regularly making $100,000 per year in gross revenue, before expenses. A study by the Economic Policy Institute found that U.S. Uber drivers make an average of $11.77 per hour after deducting Uber's fees and driver vehicle expenses from passenger fares. After a driver deducts mandatory self-employment taxes, the hourly averages decline to $10.87 per hour. The study also found that most drivers only work part-time, on average 17 hours per week, and for an average of three months a year.

In comparing traditional full-time jobs to side hustles, the Economic Policy Institute notes that a *pre-tax* wage rate of $11.77 is significantly less than the $32.06 average hourly rate of private-sector workers and the $14.99 average hourly rate for workers in the lowest-paid occupations (service occupation workers). If the average Uber driver is working 17 hours per week at a rate of $10.87 per hour, they are only making $184.89 per week or $739.16 per month for a few months a year.

The real draw for gig economy jobs is the flexibility they offer, you work when you want without committing yourself to a traditional work schedule. The pay is lower because of this convenience, but these jobs provide a supplemental income stream, which can be quite useful in the short-term, but won't replace a full-time job. In addition, with most side hustle jobs you are still trading your time for money and as we have learned, you only create real wealth when your investments/assets generate income without a commensurate requirement of your time.

Systematized Side Hustles

There are situations where you create a side hustle that generates ongoing revenue streams and develops into a true business. This would include people who have created successful blogs or videos supported by advertising and direct revenue, or people who have systematized using Airbnb for short-term rental properties and earn more revenue than traditional monthly rentals. The ability to generate income from royalties from creative works such as books, songs or photographs is also a potential side hustle that allows you to generate income multiple times from work you completed once.

Limit Your Losses

There are two upsides of starting a side hustle as a precursor to a business. The first is being able to try out various types of work without quitting your day job. You can experiment with a few different options to see which one might be the best fit. The second is having the luxury of being able to fail without derailing your broader financial freedom plans. If you are going to try to turn your hobby into a side hustle set the amount you intend to invest from the very beginning. If you decide to allocate $2,500 to a novelty t-shirt business, once the money is spent you are done. Don't add more, unless there is a clear indication that revenue is increasing, and you can become profitable. There is

171

nothing wrong with taking a risk and failing but recognize these mistakes and don't put good money after bad. Remember, lead with revenue; if you don't have profits you don't have a business, you have a hobby that costs money.

Fitting Side-Hustles into Life

Single parents responsible for younger children may not have the option of working nights or weekends, but there ways to generate revenue such as watching the children of a friend while they work a side hustle and having them watch yours while you work yours. Alternatively, you can watch the kids for a few families for a fee and that becomes your side hustle. Single parents could also look at side hustles that can be done from home such as tutoring, developing a blog, freelance writing or editing, bookkeeping, music lessons, consulting remotely, or handling customer service calls. Initially it is fine to trade time for money because you are looking to learn and develop a more entrepreneurial mindset which will lead you to future opportunities where you won't trade time for money.

Pain Points, Equal Opportunity

When it comes to finding a side hustle, it helps to identify tasks you are happy to do, which other people dislike. Their pain points such as cleaning, filing taxes, bookkeeping, or selling may be your opportunity. It is not the same as trading your time for money if you are truly enjoying the work. The pain point also works in reverse, if you abhor certain tasks, find someone who excels at them to take them off your hands. Passing off your pain points to others who enjoy them will also improve your overall happiness. This process also keeps you focused on the work where you have a comparative advantage and helps to improve efficiency.

As an example, a few years ago, I wanted to purchase a $1,500 flat screen television. The price was hard for me to justify, so I decided to come up with a side hustle to pay for it. *When you identify a goal, your brain sets to solving the puzzle and opportunities soon present themselves.* Within a few days one of my friends said he had to sell his car and he was dreading the process. I love selling, so I offered to sell it for him. After it sold, he generously gave me a gift card as a thank you and a light bulb went off. Working overseas there are many people who move regularly and need to sell their vehicles. I reached out to a few other friends looking to sell their cars and soon received enough gift cards to get the flat screen.

Spot an Opportunity: Guy with the Donuts

Being on the lookout for ways to make money often reminds me of the guy with the donuts. In Washington D.C., I worked near one of the main subway interchanges and as I exited the subway, I would see a guy selling donuts. He cleverly arranged to have 50 small boxes of donuts delivered to him at the entrance of the subway station. Having only 50 boxes gave the appearance of a limited supply. He was only there a few times a week, so his presence was a pleasant surprise. He was dressed in a suit and greeted everyone with a smile suggesting donuts would cheer up co-workers. He had a series of clever little comments to elicit a smile. He had this market figured out and quickly sold all his donuts and then went to his job nearby. I discovered he was making a profit of 50% on his donut sales. This clever entrepreneur was profiting about $400 every week or $1,600 per month before he even started his day job. He spotted an opportunity and capitalized on it. It is a great reminder to keep your eyes open so in the future you can be the guy with the donuts.

Entrepreneurship as Immediate Income

The money earned from entrepreneurial activities and side hustles is *Immediate Income* category (like Levels 1 and 2) it is immediately yours to use without age restrictions. The income grid for Levels 1-4 (all shaded gray) is below with the addition of Level 5 which is $500 per month ($6,000 per year) from an entrepreneurial endeavor like a side hustle. Over time, you should be able to grow this amount by several multiples, but $500 is our baseline. Remember an important benefit of owning a small business is the numerous tax deductions they afford. Tax deductions are not included in the grid below, but they will lower some of your daily expenses tied to your business activity.

Annual Income from Three Sample Portfolios (Level 5)

Small Portfolio	Medium Portfolio	Large Portfolio
Immediate Income (Levels 1 and 2 combined)		
$17,365	$43,150	$75,900
Middle Age Income (Level 3) Starting Age 55-67		
60% Stocks / 40% Bond with 4% withdrawal rate.		
$100,000 = $4,000	$300,000 = $12,000	$600,000 = $24,000
Senior Income (Level 4 Income) (Age 69)		
Average Social Security Benefits after 15% reduction: $14,892		

Immediate Income from Small Business/Side Hustle (Level 5)

$6,000	*$6,000*	*$6,000*

Total Annual Income Levels 1-5 combined.

$42,257	$76,042	$120,792

Key Takeaways:

• Although there is a lot of excitement about the potential for side hustles and the gig economy, the actual per hour income rates for these jobs is usually lower than traditional employment.

• Side hustles that involve creative works that you can sell repeatedly or content that generates a continuous revenue streams through sales or advertising can turn into a business and replace your day job.

• Side hustles are most effective when you can find a way to pursue your passions, so they don't feel like work. Look for a pain point for other people and create a side hustle around that task.

• If you find a way to systematize your side hustle, it will operate more like a business and you will not be trading your time for money.

• There are entrepreneurial opportunities all around us, think of the guy selling donuts near the subway; find an opportunity that appeals to you and capitalize on it.

CHAPTER 20: REAL ESTATE

Real estate is probably the most efficient way for the average person to become wealthy. Real estate investing, when done right, forgives mistakes, educates along the way, and provides four distinct benefits for obtaining financial freedom. Before we delve into these four benefits, I want to share an example of how quickly real estate can create wealth and how little money it takes to have success.

Turning $39,000 into $650,000

Leading up to the global financial crisis in 2007 we thought real estate was overpriced. Property prices were soaring, but the rents could not cover expenses, leading to a significant loss each month. Many investors were banking on appreciation from higher prices. When everyone was excited about buying, we were excited about selling. *This is a strategy called going against the herd.* People are social creatures and sometimes they move in the same direction without thinking it through. Our analysis told us that buying was the wrong direction. In response, we went the opposite way and we sold two properties and waited on the sidelines.

By 2010 real estate prices had plummeted, banks were foreclosing on properties and the herd decided real estate was a bad investment and were fleeing. Again, we disagreed with the herd as our analysis said this was the time to buy. We purchased a property for $210,000. Our down payment and closing costs were $35,000. *We had saved this money by following the steps outlined in the 10 Stages Workbook.* We then repeated the process buying another property for $195,000. Our down payment and closing costs were $39,000. We then had two properties acquired for $77,000 and the rents covered the mortgage payments and expenses allowing us to generate a profit.

Within a few years, real estate prices recovered and both properties appreciated. We did a cash out refinance on the first property pulling out the $35,000 down payment we used to buy it. Now we have $0 of our own money in the property. Cash out refinancing is a great way to recycle your down payment for your next property. Fast forward a few more years and the first property is valued at $480,000 with a loan balance of $160,000 leaving us with $320,000 in equity plus the monthly rental income. The second property is worth $410,000 with a loan balance of $80,000. Our equity is $320,000 plus the monthly rental income.

For the $39,000 that remains invested, we have $650,000 in equity. It can take a lifetime to save $650,000 but with real estate, you can earn this amount with a couple of signatures and a relatively manageable down payment. The annual rental income from these two properties is nearly twice the salary of my first job and well above our initial $39,000 investment. Put simply, this is why real estate creates millionaires and why real estate must be part of your long-term investment plan.

Four Benefits of Real Estate

Real estate is so effective at creating wealth because it has four distinct benefits. First, the rents from a tenant creates positive cash flow, which is monthly income after all the property expenses are paid. This is money you can reinvest or use to pay your personal expenses.

Second is appreciation, which is the increasing value of the property as shown in the example of the two properties we purchased. *But, treat appreciation like a bonus; do not count on it, because prices may fall again.* Never purchase a property if you are basing your returns on assumed appreciation. If values decline and the investment can't support itself from the rents it may result in a loss.

The third benefit is loan amortization, which is the process of paying down the mortgage over the life of the loan. You are using your tenant's rent to pay the mortgage. Each mortgage payment consists of principal, interest, taxes and insurance (PITI). In the first few years of the loan, your payments are mostly interest and in the last few years, they are mostly principal. If you look at a loan amortization chart online, you will see how this process works. Each payment of principal increases the equity you have in the property as well as your net worth.

The fourth benefit of real estate is tax shelter, which comes in the form of depreciation. *Depreciation is unlike other real estate expenses because you don't actually pay money out of pocket for it.* Depreciation is a tax deduction offered by the government based on drawing down the usable life of the property. Depreciation only applies to the physical buildings and certain closing costs, but not to the land underneath the property. Here is an example on how depreciation works:

Enoch buys a single-family home for $200,000. The house is worth $160,000 and the land is worth $40,000. Since Enoch can't depreciate the land, he takes the price of the house and combines it with $2,000 in eligible closing costs to find his basis of $162,000 for the property. Enoch divides the basis by 27.5 years, which is the depreciation formula set by the U.S. government for residential property. He finds he can deduct $5,891 in depreciation on his taxes each year for the next 27.5 years. Here are those numbers again as a formula:
Purchase price $200,000 – $40,000 (land) + $2,000 (closing costs) = $162,000 (basis) / 27.5 = $5,891

Enoch will list the $5,891 as a depreciation expense on his federal tax return and it will offset his rental profits. If he made $5,981 in rental profit before depreciation, he would owe $0 in tax on his rental income. Is rental income starting to look better than the income from your job? If he made $6,000 in profit, he would only owe $109 in tax. This is a fantastic way to shelter your rental income from taxes.

Nevertheless, as much as the government likes to give, it also likes to take away. The government will want to recapture this generous gift of depreciation when you sell the property. This is called a recapture tax because the government is recapturing the tax on the depreciation it allowed you to use as an expense. Enoch might pay a recapture tax of 25% on the amount he depreciated, so when he sells the property, he will owe $1,483 in recapture tax on the $5,891 in depreciation he used. If he took depreciation for ten years and had $58,910 in depreciation expenses, he would owe $14,830 in recapture tax when he sells the property.

Fortunately, there are ways to defer paying these recapture taxes as well as capital gains taxes discussed in chapter 5 by using a 1031 exchange which is covered on the LoadedforLife website. Explaining a 1031 exchange is beyond the scope of this chapter. Also please check your country's tax laws regarding depreciation and recapture taxes for real estate investments.

Rental Property Expenses

In addition to deductions for mortgage interest and depreciation, you will also be able to deduct various expenses related to operating your rental property including advertising, repairs, property taxes, commissions, professional fees, supplies, cleaning, insurance, and utilities. To estimate repairs use 5% of the monthly rents. It helps to make a list of these anticipated expenses on a spreadsheet to get a better sense of the cost of owning a property before you buy. Compare the expenses to the rental income to see if the property will generate a profit or a loss. If you are looking at a realtor's listing sheet for a property it will list some of these expenses, but double check these figures, as they are not always accurate.

You can also check county records for property taxes and utility companies for utility rates. Call an insurer for an insurance quote based on the specifications of the property. A mortgage calculator will provide expected interest costs for a loan. Also keep in mind that expenses like property taxes and insurance tend to increase each year and if rents are not also rising it can make the property less profitable.

Three Expenses: Common Mistakes

Newer real estate investors often make mistakes on three types of expenses which are property management, vacancies, and future capital expenses. Check with property managers in your area to see what they charge to manage a property. Fees are often between 8-10% of monthly rents. Ask about any additional expenses such as lease renewal fees or new tenant fees as these increase the cost of property management and consume your profits. Even if you plan to manage the property yourself, account for property management on your list of expenses. Situations change and you may not be able to manage the property and must hire professional management. A property needs to be profitable with property management as one of the expenses.

Vacancies

Factor in a vacancy rate equal to five percent of the annual rents. If a property rents for $1,000 a month the monthly vacancy reserve is $50. Have a vacancy reserve even if there is high demand for rentals because markets change and demand may decline. Great rental markets can saturate from overbuilding. Beware of too many construction cranes building apartment buildings; they are the first indication of future saturation. Vacancies can quickly turn your rental returns from a profit to a loss and sustained vacancies, especially if you have multiple properties, can derail your entire financial plan.

Capital Expenses

Your budget should also include a line item equal to five percent of monthly rents to pay for capital improvements like a new roof, sewer lines or heating/cooling system. If you need to pay $8,000 for a new roof that was not budgeted for, you have probably wiped out your rental profits for a year or more.

If you buy an older property, it can be advantageous to make major repairs to kitchens, bathrooms, plumbing, electrical, and the roof all at once. You can also upgrade all the appliances as well. A refreshed property in excellent condition is likely to generate higher rents, and avoids the hassle of fixing a series of repairs over the first few years which makes managing the property easier.

So as a quick recap these are three often overlooked expenses you will want to factor in when assessing properties to buy:

* Property Management = 8-10% of monthly rent

* Vacancies = 5% of monthly rent

* Capital expenses = 5% of rent

How to Quickly Value Properties

We have covered the four benefits of investing in properties and the types of expenses to expect when owning a property. The next step is to learn how to assess whether a property might be a good investment. As a real estate investor, you will look at dozens of properties at a time, so you need a few basic formulas for comparing properties.

1. Cost Per Square Foot: Divide the total price of the property by the square footage. A $120,000 property that is 1,200 square feet is $100 per square foot. If you find a property selling for $80 per square foot in the same area it may be a deal. You are looking for the outliers, properties priced lower for some reason. It

could be due to a motivated seller or as simple as the realtor making a mistake when entering the data of the listing.

2. Gross Rent Yield: If you divide the annual rents by the cost of the property, you find the gross rent yield. For example, a property renting for $1,000 a month ($12,000 a year) that costs $100,000 has a gross rent yield of 12%. If you compare the gross rent yield of two similar properties it may indicate which one provides a better return. Sometimes properties in a less expensive part of the town will generate a higher rate of return in rents.

3. The 1% Rule: The 1% percent rule means that the monthly rent for a property is equal to 1% of its purchase price. A $70,000 property would rent for $700 per month. Higher quality residential properties tend to have a rent yield below 1%. Nice single-family homes in a good neighborhood may only have a rent yield of .8%. Just because the rent is below the 1% rule does not mean the property is a bad investment, there are other factors to consider described in more detail later in the chapter.

4. Cash Flow Per Door: After all expenses, including mortgage interest, vacancies, property management and capital expenses, the rental income left over is the cash flow. Some investors try to hit a certain target such as $100 in cash flow per door. Some areas might generate a higher rate of cash flow such as $200 or $300 per door. Again, it all depends on the location and the type of property. Multifamily properties are more likely to have a higher cash per door as you are spreading the expenses over a larger number of units.

5. Capitalization Rate: The capitalization rate, usually referred to as "cap rate" is a common tool for comparing commercial real estate. To find the cap rate, first add up all the operating expenses for the property for a year, which include taxes, insurance, maintenance, and estimated repairs. *It does not include the*

costs associated with acquiring the property or the financing costs of the loan, as these are not operating expenses. Second, take the expected annual rents and subtract the operating expenses to find the net operating income. Third, divide the net operating income by the purchase price of the property to find the cap rate. See the example below:

Cap Rate Example:
You find a warehouse for sale for $100,000 that rents for $12,000 per year. The annual operating expenses are $4,000 per year. The rent of $12,000 – $4,000 in operating expenses = $8,000 in net operating income. Divide $8,000 in net operating income by the $100,000 purchase price = 8% cap rate. You can compare the cap rate of this warehouse to a second warehouse with a cap rate of 9.5% to see which might be a better investment. There may be other factors to look at to determine the best investment, but the cap rate is a good starting point.

Real Estate Niche

There are many ways to invest in real estate. You can purchase buy and hold single-family homes or multifamily properties, you can fix and flip homes or invest in commercial properties, mobile home parks or self-storage units. You can invest in expensive A-class desirable neighborhoods or less expensive properties in C-class neighborhoods that may be less desirable. What is important is to find the right niche for your personality. If you don't like having difficult conversations or have a hard time sticking to your rules, you will want to consider hiring a property manager. You must enforce the terms of your lease with your tenants. If you think of every property you buy as your own home and become angry if tenants don't take perfect care of it, you may need to find a partner who handles this aspect of the business.

Things will go wrong, properties suffer damage, and you will encounter difficult tenants even after diligent screening. Don't invest in a neighborhood you are afraid to visit and don't invest your entire nest egg in one deal that leaves you sleepless because your entire net worth is wrapped up in it. Know yourself and invest accordingly. The goal is to purchase real estate that allows you to sleep at night. *Remember the core tenant of this book is creating wealth and maximizing happiness. If your investments are having the opposite effect, you need to revise your investment strategy.*

Two Sample Investments

Below are two examples of potential property investments. This is to apply what you have learned in this chapter and to show you how to identify possible positive and negative factors for each property.

Location 1: Nice single-family homes costing $200,000 and renting for $1,500 per month. The rents are below the 1% rule and the gross rent yield is 9%. When you run the numbers on all your expenses (including vacancies, capital expenses and property management), you will earn $75 a month in cash flow. Notice a major repair could eat your profit for the entire year. This is an A-class neighborhood near excellent schools and shopping. A state park surrounds the neighborhood prohibiting any future large-scale residential construction, thus limiting supply. This is a good thing.

There are new employers moving in and creating higher paying jobs, some within walking distance of this property. Your research shows these homes are appreciating from an average of $165,000 two years ago to $185,000 last year. Projected prices for next year are $215,000. Properties sell quickly, often for above asking price and some buyers pay in cash. As you walk the neighborhood and talk to neighbors, you learn that renters stay for five or seven years and rental vacancies fill quickly because of the excellent schools.

Location 2: Single family homes costing $70,000 and renting for $1,000 per month. The neighborhood has higher than average crime rates and fewer employment opportunities but there is good access to public transport. This is more of a C-class neighborhood but is quite livable. Estimated monthly expenses including mortgage costs are $750 resulting in $250 in cash flow. You learn that rental properties turn over every year or two and there is usually a one-month vacancy. Your proposed 5% annual vacancy reserve of $600 may get used quickly. You talk to property managers in the area and they say properties frequently need $1,000 in cleaning and repairs after each tenant. You suggest adding a $500 cleaning fee to your lease, but the property managers warn you that the standard for cleaning fees is $100 and tenants may not sign a lease with a $500 fee.

Sales data shows homes in this neighborhood were selling for $66,000 three years ago, so appreciation is slow. Real estate agents advise that some sellers will offer seller financing at reasonable rates in order to sell their home, which would allow you to avoid some of the fees of a traditional bank loan. There are also some motivated sellers in the neighborhood who might be willing to accept an offer a few thousand dollars below the asking price. Remember the example of Sharon who was looking for options to earn $5,000 instead of working for a promotion; some of those options are here.

Analysis: Which of these is the better investment? It depends on your temperament and your preferred real estate niche. It also depends on whether you have capital available and the good credit necessary to get traditional financing. Are you looking for immediate cash flow or are you willing to break even for a few years for a nicer property? In location 2 if you can get a property for $60,000 that is in comparable shape to those properties selling for $70,000 you would have immediate equity in the deal. If you can line up seller financing, you might be able to save a few thousand dollars in bank fees and avoid making a large down payment.

However, motivated sellers are not just in less desirable neighborhoods, you may also find a motivated seller or seller financing in location 1. In either location, you might find a 3-bedroom property to convert to a 4-bedroom allowing you to increase the monthly rents. In location 2 if you had a tenant that was taking good care of the property you could offer them $100 to sign the lease for another year to reduce your vacancy costs.

The key point to understand is that either of these investments could be quite profitable, it depends on your ability to creatively increase your return. As I said earlier in this book, everything is negotiable, and you don't get what you do't ask for. *You are more likely to negotiate a great deal than to just find one waiting of you.*

If you want a little more information about investing in real estate please see the article Ten Things to Know About Real Estate Investing on LoadedforLife.com

Key Takeaways:

• If you have the desire to become a millionaire, one of the best ways to achieve this goal is by investing in real estate.

• Going against the herd can be a valuable strategy, sell when others are buying and buy when others are selling. But make sure your analysis supports this strategy.

• The four benefits for creating wealth with real estate are cash flow, appreciation, loan amortization, and tax shelter (depreciation).

• Among your real estate expenses, pay close attention to estimated repairs, property management, vacancies, and capital expenses. Neglecting these expenses is a common mistake for newer investors.

• Real estate is local, so get to know the area where you plan to invest. Use the various strategies discussed for analyzing properties such as the price per square foot, rent per square foot and rent yield, the 1% rule, cash flow per door, and cap rate. Find a real estate niche that matches your skills and temperament.

• The article Ten Things to Know About Real Estate Investing on the website Loaded for Life advises you to set aside $2,000 in reserves for each property you buy and keep track of rent yields as an indicator that a real estate bubble is occurring. Also watch for oversupply of new properties, which can increase vacancy rates. Get adequate insurance to protect your assets, and purchasing multifamily properties can help you scale faster.

• The article also states that owning five properties will cover your *Basic Living Expenses Budget* and eventually most of your *Lifestyle Expenses Budget.* Use creative financing to purchase real estate because a good deal can always find financing. Properly vet every tenant and follow the landlord/tenant laws in your area and get everything related to real estate in writing.

CHAPTER 21: MEASURING PERFORMANCE

Success and Mistakes, Leave an Evidence Trail

At this point you understand the importance of tracking your spending and creating multiple income streams, the next step is to begin tracking your progress. This is a significant but sometimes overlooked part of creating wealth. *You have to measure performance to truly hold yourself accountable.* Tracking key data points such as annual savings rate, net worth, and investment returns provides a clear picture of your results and identifies which assets are driving your success. You can use the data to revise your strategies and better optimize your results.

The process also provides positive reinforcement for your efforts, you become more motivated as you hit financial milestones and reduce the number of years left until you reach your goals. There are five numbers to track as your personal finance dashboard:

1) Monthly spending rate;
2) Annual savings rate;
3) Net worth;
4) Rental property tracker for income and expenses;
5) Monthly income streams and your three budgets from chapter 13.

Monthly Spending

We covered the process of tracking your monthly spending in chapter 7 and explained how this process will help you spend less by being more conscious of how you spend and retraining your brain to spend wisely.

Annual Savings Rate

You can track your annual savings rate at the end of the year or on a specific date like when you file your income taxes. You can keep these records in a basic spreadsheet, or use one of the various online budgeting tools, or a simple pen and paper. Whatever option is easiest for you. The process is relatively easy. First, list all your income for the year including any employer matching funds in a retirement account. Second, list all taxes paid at the federal, state, and local level and subtract it from your income. The difference is your *after-tax* income and is what you had available for living expenses and investing.

Third, add up the amount you saved for the year. Savings includes cash, money invested, or money used to pay down good debt. Also include funds contributed to pre-tax retirement accounts plus any employer match. Don't include payments such as repairs to your rental properties or paying off bad debt like a car loan, these are expenses.

Fourth, divide your *after-tax* income by the amount you saved to find your *after-tax* savings rate. For example, if you save $10,000 and divide this by your *after-tax* income of $40,000 your savings rate is 25%. Make a concerted effort to increase your savings rate, even if just slightly, every year. This process is also a great tool for seeing where your money goes when broken down between the three categories of taxes, savings and expenses. *It is can be an incentive to find ways to lower your taxes so you can convert the difference to savings.*

Example of David's tracking annual savings rate:

Chart on next page

David's Annual Savings Rate

Income

Paid income (W-2)	$52,000 (includes $12,000 401(k) contribution and employer match)
Savings Interest	$ 50 ($5,000 in emergency fund)
Stock Dividends	$ 650
Bonds	$ 300
Notes	$ 1,000
Side hustle	$ 4,000
Rental income	$ 4,000 (roommate rent, less expenses and depreciation)
Total income	**$62,000** (401k contribution and employer match are not taxed)
Total Taxes	**$10,000** (includes Federal and State taxes)
Total After-Tax Income	**$52,000** (funds available for living expenses and saving)

Savings

Savings	$ 500 (added to emergency fund)
Savings	$ 4,000 (paid extra principal payment on mortgage)
Savings	$ 2,000 (401k employer match)
Savings	$10,000 (401k contributions)
Savings	$ 5,000 (Roth IRA contributions)
Total Saved	**$21,500** (Expenses were $30,500 for the year)
After-tax savings rate:	**41.3%**

When we started our plan for financial freedom we initially saved between a quarter and a third of our income. After we were married and created other income streams, we saved more than half of our income. Within a few years, we were living on less than one salary (with two kids) and investing the rest. We were living well below our means by not falling into the life-style inflation trap.

Most importantly, our savings rate was driven even higher because our investments were creating annual income which we immediately reinvested. This is the snowball effect of your investments creating more wealth. As you pay down the good debt on your assets your monthly liabilities decline which increases your monthly cash flow. Each year as this cash flow climbs your are rapidly reducing your reliance on your day job.

Tracking Net Worth

At a minimum, track your net worth twice a year to have a

detailed understanding of your financial situation. Regularly reviewing your net worth enables you to keep a running list of mini goals for the next few months. These goals might include a reminder to raise the rent on a property or to refinance a property to take cash out or to increase your investments in a particular asset class that is performing well. You will see which investments are generating the best returns and increasing your net worth. If you don't track these figures you cheat yourself of this valuable data which improves decision making.

When calculating your net worth, you can use a spreadsheet or one of many online tools or apps such as Mint, YNAB (You Need a Budget), or Personal Capital. Regardless of the tool you use, make sure to only include assets, as defined in chapter 9, in your net worth. Include your primary residence, but not personal property. See Samantha's example below for tracking net worth.

Samantha's Net Worth

Asset	Value	Minus Debt	Net value
Primary residence	$130,000	-$80,000	$50,000
Rental property 1	$80,000	-$70,000	$10,000
50% ownership of Rental property 2	$40,000 (50% of value)	-$25,000	$15,000
401k	$40,000	$0	$40,000
Roth IRA	$15,000	$0	$15,000
Emergency Fund	$ 5,000	$0	$ 5,000
Checking account	$ 6,500	$0	$ 6,500
Reserves for real estate repairs	$ 3,000	$0	$ 3,000
Reserves for vacancies	$ 1,000		
Real Estate Notes	$ 3,500	$0	$ 3,500
Equity investment in a startup	$ 2,000	$0	$ 2,000
Total Net Worth			*$150,000*

Rental Property Tracker

Your rental property tracker lists the rent for each property as well as the monthly mortgage payment consisting of principal, interest, taxes and insurance (PITI). Also include the gross rent yield which, as you will remember from chapter 20, is the annual rent divided by the cost basis of the property. You can also list the cost of property management for each property. This rental property tracker is not designed to track all your rental property expenses; these will need to be kept on a spreadsheet for each individual property for completing your annual taxes.

The purpose of a rental property tracker is to provide a dashboard of how each property is performing. The rent yield shows which properties are generating higher yields and are likely more profitable. See Malcolm's sample rental property tracker below along with a detailed explanation for each property:

Malcolm's Monthly Rental Property Tracker

Property	Basis	Monthly Rent	Gross Rent Yield	PITI	Property MGT	Net Revenue
A	$125,000	$1,000	9.6%	$700	$0	$300
B	$200,000	$2,000	12%	$1,400	$200	$400
C	$150,000	$1,300	10.4%	$300	$130	$870
D	$280,000	$2,000	8.5%	$1,600	$0	$400
E	$140,000	$1,800	15.4%	$950	$0	$850
Totals		$8,100		$4,925	$330	$2,820

Property A is Malcolm's primary residence with a roommate providing $1,000 per month in rent. There are no property management expenses. Malcolm is living for free, plus making $300 in monthly income. He has a 30-year fixed rate mortgage which provides a lower monthly payment. If Malcolm moves out, he can rent his bedroom to a tenant and increase his total return on the property. Malcolm is also building equity, as a portion of each mortgage payment includes principal which reduces his loan.

Property B is an investment property with a 15-year fixed rate mortgage, so Malcolm's payments are higher than with a 30-year mortgage, but the property will be paid off sooner. This property is building equity at a faster rate, but Malcolm is giving up some cash flow in the short-term. This property is far away, so Malcolm pays 10% of the rents for property management.

Property C is paid off, so the expenses are only for taxes and insurance. Malcolm could refinance this property to purchase another property with cash. However, he likes having this property paid off to reduce his overall debt and risk levels. Malcolm also pays 10% of the rents for property management.

<u>Property D</u> was bought in a nice neighborhood in walking distance to excellent schools. Homes are expensive in the neighborhood and the rent is not as profitable. Malcolm bought the property because he hopes to have a family and eventually live there. In the meantime, Malcolm's tenant is paying off the mortgage for him. Buying real estate is not always about the money, sometimes it is like playing chess, you make a move now hoping to yield benefits later in the game.

<u>Property E</u> is a small property Malcolm bought in his first job so he could walk to work. When he changed jobs, he rented this property, and bought his current property because it was close to his job and he could continue walking to work. This saves him the expense of having a car. As rents increased over time, Malcolm is earning a high rent yield on this property.

Income Stream Tracker

The income stream tracker is the Level 1-5 income grid for tracking your *Immediate Income, Middle Age Income* and *Senior Income.* It includes all your investments, entrepreneurial ventures or side hustles, and payments from annuities, pensions, and social security. It also lists the estimates for your three key budgets: *Basic Living Expenses Budget, Lifestyle Expenses Budget* and *Longevity Expenses Budget.*

Chart on next page

Immediate Income Assets:

	Amount	**Yearly Income**
Long term treasuries ___% return)	$_____	$_____
1-year CDs ___% return	$_____	$_____
Corporate Bonds ___% withdrawal rate	$_____	$_____
Stocks ___% withdrawal rate	$_____	$_____
Private Equity Shares ___% return	$_____	$_____
MLPs ___% return	$_____	$_____
REITs ___% return	$_____	$_____
Mortgaged Rental Property	Annual Rents	$_____
Paid off Rental Property	Annual Rents	$_____
Peer to Peer Lending ____% Return	$_____	$_____
Hard Money Loan ___% Return	$_____	$_____
Notes ___% Return)	$_____	$_____
Small Business	Business income	$_____
Side Hustle	Side Hustle income	$_____

Total Immediate Income per year $_____
(Immediate Income available at any age)

Middle Age Income Assets:

	Amount	Yearly Income
Tax Deferred 401(k)Account ____% withdrawal rate	$_____	$_____
Tax Deferred IRA ____% withdrawal rate	$_____	$_____
Roth IRA ____% withdrawal rate	$_____	$_____

Total Middle Age Income Per Year $_____
(Income available at age 55 to 59½ and older)

Senior Income Assets:

	Amount	Yearly Income
Annuities	Age it begins _____	$_____
Pension	Age it begins _____	$_____
Government Superannuation	Age it begins _____	$_____
Social Security Retirement Benefits With an anticipated 15% reduction of benefit 	Age it begins _____	$_____

Total Senior Income Per Year $_____

Three Budgets:

Include your three budgets from chapter 13 below. These serve as a guide to keep you focused on your financial targets and to see how close you are to covering your relevant expenses.

Basic Living Expenses Budget $_____

Lifestyle Expenses Budget $_____

Longevity Expenses Budget $_____

Key Takeaways:

• Hold yourself accountable by measuring your performance. Track key data points such as your annual savings rate, net worth, and investment returns for a clear picture of your performance.

• Identify which assets are contributing to your success to better optimize your results.

• Tracking progress serves as positive reinforcement for your efforts. Your personal finance dashboard should track your monthly spending rate, net worth, annual savings rate, rental property income and expenses, and your various income streams broken down between *Immediate Income, Middle Age Income* and *Senior Income.*

• Keep track of your three key budgets from chapter 13 to see how close you are to achieving financial freedom.

CHAPTER 22: ADVICE FOR DOING BUSINESS

This chapter will focus on general advice and a few strategies for doing business, building contacts, and actively listening to people. Some of these suggestions are drawn from our own successes or mistakes and from watching other investors. If you can learn from another person's mistake without paying the financial penalty it is the equivalent of a free education. Similarly you want to emulate those who are performing at a level you hope to reach.

Sounds Like a Steal

At times you will find investment opportunities with an incredible upside potential. This may be an undervalued property from an owner willing to discount the price because they are ready to move on in life. Or it could be becoming a partner in a business that you can change to become far more profitable. However, you must do your due diligence with every investment to verify your assumptions before you buy.

The first property I tried to buy was an apartment that was offered below market price. The seller said he was not using a realtor and by saving this 6% commission he could offer a lower price. This sounded reasonable, but he was particularly interested in receiving a deposit from me to hold the property and he wanted a cash sale. Instead, I offered to give the deposit to an attorney who would help with the transaction. I also paid to run a title search on the property to see if it was free of any liens or debts.

It turned out the property had tax liens twice the value of the property. This seller was looking for a deposit which he would never return and a cash sale because he was hoping to trick someone into buying his property with the attached tax liens. Tax liens stay on the property when you buy it. If I had not done my due diligence, I would have inherited his tax problems.

Be cautious of any investments offered below market value, unless you have negotiated the discount. Also beware of anyone who claims to consistently beat the market average. Sometimes sellers will falsify rental income reports to make a property more profitable to justify an inflated sales price. Any potential investment could be a scam regardless of the reputation of the person presenting the offer. Bernie Madoff was very well respected on Wall Street and thought to be a genius until he proved to be a criminal running a Ponzi scheme. Some very smart people, who should have known better, lost millions of dollars investing with him.

The desire to become wealthy sometimes encourages us to lower our guard. I knew a person who lost more than half a million dollars on an investment in the Caribbean that turned out to be scam. If he had spent a few thousand dollars to fly down and personally check on the status of his investment he would have avoided these losses. He was relying on photos being sent showing the work being done on the project, unfortunately the photos were of someone else's project. *Trust, but verify.*

Similarly, don't invest in anything that is so complex you really don't understand it. In the lead up to the global financial crisis there were people investing in derivatives and aspects of collateralized debt obligations they could not comprehend and therefore could not properly gauge the risk. *If you can't explain an investment in under a minute to a friend, you should probably not invest in it.*

Trusted Advice

In chapter 12 on creating wealth, an emphasis was placed on building a team of experts to provide you with the right technical advice. Success comes from having a network of people who are similarly driven to achieve their goals. Ideas need constructive feedback to focus them and make them better. This network becomes a virtuous cycle, you help others to achieve their goals as they help you with yours.

Renowned businessman Jim Rohn is famous for saying you are the average of the five people with whom you spend the most time. Are the five people you spend most of your time with people who are positive and motivated? Do your five people seek to be helpful and supportive? If not, you may need to start changing your five people. *It is better to spend time alone than with the wrong people.*

I have a long-time friend who has graciously provided sound advice over the years. He will listen to an idea and respond with an honest assessment. Early on in our investing career we considered doing an elaborate remodel of a 1920s house in the United States while living in Africa. My friend looked over the proposal, immediately noting that I had not yet lined up a proven and trusted contractor. He advised that once I opened the walls of such an old house there was no telling what I would find and how much it would cost to fix. He took a deep breath and his advice was brilliant, *"Nate, there are television shows dedicated to warn people not to do what you are about to do. Wait until you are back on this side of the globe and do the project then."* He was absolutely right, this was great advice. He saved us from a lot of stress. We deferred the project and put the money into a different investment that was much easier to manage from overseas.

Seeking Advice

Seek advice from people who possess actual and legitimate experience in a subject. Ask a mechanic about your car and a lawyer about the law, not the other way around. Over the years, we have had several people who have never owned a rental property tell us it is only a way to lose money. You can just smile and politely change the subject. Do not give random opinions the same value as advice from experienced experts.

Asking Questions

As we were preparing for a rafting trip in Africa, I looked on a distant riverbank and saw a small four-foot-long crocodile. Some might turn to the guide and ask, "Is that a crocodile?" which confirms what you already know. I started chatting with our guide and while blocking it from his view, I asked are there are *any crocodiles* in the river. He shook his head and said "no". Now, I know two things. There are crocodiles in the river, at least small ones. And far more important, I know my guide's advice is unreliable. I much prefer to know this *before* we start out on the river and need to rely on this guide's advice.

The Two-Way Street

When someone has been kind enough to share their valuable time, be sure to respond with a gesture that lets them know you appreciate it. This gesture could be a small gift or something you think this person might need. The act and the thought are more important than the price. At a minimum, provide them with a gift card for their favorite restaurant tucked in a hand-written note. I am amazed when I see a very busy person spend an hour or two mentoring a new investor, providing very valuable advice, and the recipient disappears failing to ever express any appreciation. That may be the last time this new investor gets advice from that expert. Also, other experts will notice what happened and be less inclined to help this person in the future.

If you are a new investor, don't go back to a person seeking additional advice if you have not followed through on the original advice they provided. It shows you are not serious. It indicates you are a person who likes to talk but does not actually follow through, and that is just wasting their time.

We have all known those acquaintances who show up out of the blue seeking help or advice only to disappear until they need something again. They may be nice people but the relationship is about taking care of their needs. A kind response is to draw their attention to this pattern as they may not realize it. If it happens again after you have told them, it is best to ease these folks out of your life. They believe the relationship is a one-way street, let them find someone else to rely on.

What You Say, Write and Sign

It takes years to build a reputation and minutes to lose it. The emergence of social media allows people to turn a flippant comment into a viral fail. To paraphrase Mitch Ratcliffe, with the advent of the internet and social media, mistakes haven't be able to accelerate this fast since combining tequila with handguns.

In law school one of my professors would say, "Think of every document you sign as exhibit A in the lawsuit against you, and think how your words will sound when they are read out by the judge to a room full of people." This is great advice and something to keep in mind before you send an angry email, sign a contract without closely reading it, or lose your temper in an argument.

We all make mistakes and if you make the wrong call and must eat your words you want to make sure they were sweet. Be professional, be diplomatic, and if you are writing something that may not be received well by the recipient, make sure you read it with a calm head before you send it.

Assume Positive Intent

When it comes to dealing with people both professionally and in your personal life, *assume positive intent until proven otherwise.* People may not communicate in the way they intended so you need to confirm their intent before assuming it is bad. Go back calmy seeking clarification, otherwise you will unnecessarily escalate the situation. When people think communications have soured they are rarely searching for helpful solutions.

Also, there may be key facts pertaining to the situation that, if known, would change your perspective. You may be working with someone who is a top performer but is facing a tragic situation in their homelife that has taken their focus. If you are dealing with them for the first time, you may mistakenly assume they are being curt or are a poor performer, but a little context would change your opinion.

Keep Your Word

Always keep your word; it is as simple as doing what you say you will do, regardless of whether it costs you money. If you lose money, it is the cost of tuition for this lesson. Opportunity favors people who are reliable, trustworthy, and act decisively. You will make up any losses you incur for keeping your word on future investments. Also, you don't have to win big on every deal, leave some meat on the bone for other investors and you will do better in the long run. Investors don't do repeat deals if they walk away feeling cheated, and they will probably tell everyone about their negative experience working with you.

Beware of the 7 Series

A friend of mine meets regularly for breakfast with a group of seasoned investors in their late sixties and seventies. At thirty years their junior, my friend wisely listens far more than he speaks. The discussions are a wealth of knowledge and my friend periodically picks up the entire tab for breakfast, ensuring future invitations.

During a breakfast one of the investors said he was looking to sell an expensive property and met a potential buyer, described as, "a young investor in a new BMW 7 Series". The rest of the table broke into a knowing laugh, with one investor commenting "Beware of the 7 Series". Each of these investors had dealt with this type of investor before, a person who puts all their money into a luxury car to create the impression of wealth and success. These seasoned investors have come to learn that this type of buyer is never able to close on a deal because they can't come up with the money. A wiser investor would put this money into an investment, not an expensive new car. Incidentally, my friend looked out the window and noticed for the first time that every investor at the table, all multimillionaires, drove either a basic sedan or a simple pickup truck all about 10 years old.

The 7 series example relates to what economists call signaling. A common example of positive signaling is a new college graduate with a high grade point average. The degree and the grades are intended to signal to potential employers that this person has the intelligence and work ethic to be a great employee. The 7 series investor mistakenly believes the car sends a signal of success and credibility.

In reality, the new investor is engaging in what is called negative signaling. The seasoned investor views purchasing a $100,000 luxury vehicle as foolish, knowing the money is better spent on an investment. Hence, the seasoned investor is now wary of the new investor. The 7 series has brought the opposite of the desired result. As you become a more active investor think about your actions and the positive or negative signals they may be sending to those around you.

Watch for the Reveal

I have found signaling, both positive and negative, to be tremendously helpful tools. Signals help to assess credibility and authenticity, but there is one other clue I look for in conversations. I have interviewed thousands of people over the years, and I have learned that when a person loses focus on the persona they are hoping to convey, for just a second or two, they can send a remarkably powerful signal. It is usually negative, and I call it the reveal. The reveal can be a very subtle micro expression or a subtle remark, so you must watch very closely or you will miss it.

One way to facilitate the reveal is to embrace the silence in a discussion or negotiation. People tend to be uncomfortable with long pauses when nothing is being said. The desire to move past this stage may force the reveal. I also find that once a person has made the reveal, they become cognizant of it and become noticeably more cautious or nervous. This may be a shift in their body language or posture or their speech pattern; they may slow their rate of speech hoping not to make the same mistake again or speed it up hoping to get past it. This only confirms you just witnessed the reveal. There are times in conversations when it happens, and my wife will look at me and smile as we both just saw it.

In one example, I spent close to an hour talking with a potential investor and we were beginning to wrap up. I could tell he was feeling great about the discussion and I think it caused him to let his guard down. He made a comment, boasting about his knowledge on a completely unrelated subject. Unfortunately for him, it is a subject I know extremely well. My brain grabbed the reveal and said, "there it is!" The statement was so fundamentally false, that I knew the last hour was a staged performance. I smiled and shook hands not letting on what I just learned. After the meeting I ran a background check on this person and found he was a career criminal. One small comment, the reveal, was the most critical piece of information in an hour-long conversation. If I had not been watching for it, I could have missed it.

Key Takeaways:

- If it sounds like a steal, you will end up being a victim. Verify investments before you commit any money. Greed lowers your guard and even world class finance experts were tricked by Bernie Madoff's Ponzi scheme.

- Ask questions in a way the yields the most information, don't just confirm what you already know. Find out about the guide and the crocodiles.

- Be careful with what you say, write and sign. Think about how it will sound read out to your community or in a courtroom.

- Assume positive intent from the people around you unless you see clear evidence otherwise.

- Protect your credibility and do what you say you will do even if it costs you money. Opportunity favors people who are reliable, trustworthy, and act decisively. Show appreciation to those who have spent time mentoring you or helping you solve a problem.

- Watch for positive and negative signaling to assess opportunities and ensure you are sending the correct message to potential partners or investors.

- Watch for the reveal during discussions and particularly in negotiations; it will happen quickly as a micro expression or a comment and is the most important piece of information in the conversation.

CHAPTER 23: ECONOMIC TRENDS AND TAXES

Monitor Economic Cycles

Markets work in cycles, like the Biblical story of the seven fat years and seven lean years. Regardless of whether the assets are real estate, stocks, businesses or gold there are periods of strong bull markets followed by bear markets. The last serious bear market for stocks ran from October 2007 through March 2009 and values fell by 57%. This also coincided with a historic decline in real estate prices. There will also be periodic corrections, marked by a 10% decline in asset values.

When an asset class has been on a positive run for more than seven years, prepare for a possible correction by setting aside extra cash to buy when asset prices fall. This approach is not about trying to time the market for a quick profit as none of us has a crystal ball to predict the future. This approach is about paying attention to the broader trends when you invest and being prepared to profit from them. For a great example of how economic cycles work, watch the YouTube video How the Economic Machine Works by billionaire Ray Dalio.

Irrational Thinking Precedes the Crash

If the prices of an asset class cannot be justified by the underlying numbers, stop acquiring the asset class. For example, the valuations of technology stocks were astronomically high prior to their crash in late 1999. Yet many stock analysts tried to justify these ridiculous valuations. Similarly, real estate valuations in 2007 couldn't be reasonably justified. The prices of houses in desirable locations were jumping $50,000 in a matter of months. People will seek to justify irrational thinking, saying, "this is just how it is now." They will say "it is the new normal". This flawed thinking led people to buy houses they could not afford, assuming house values would continue to rise.

This Time Is Different

Along with irrational thinking, there will be other warning signs as an asset bubble builds. Sir John Templeton said the four most expensive words in the English language are, "this time it's different." This is sage advice that will apply to the next major bubble and asset crash. Also, watch out for key phrases used by news analysts or other investors, including "this market has changed" or "the old methods of pricing don't apply" or "despite the record high prices, we think there is still a potential to justify even higher valuations." Whether the market is gold, real estate or stocks, these phrases are the harbinger of bad things to come.

Also, if a particular investment like technology stocks, cryptocurrencies or vacation rentals becomes a common source of conversation at social events, it is time for caution. Nearly everyone at parties talked like tech stock experts from 1997-1999 prior to the crash. There were also media images showing everyone getting rich investing in tech stocks. The brokerage firm E-Trade had commercials about their clients having money coming "out the wazoo" and even joked in a $2 million Super Bowl commercial, pointlessly featuring two men and a chimpanzee clapping, that they had just wasted millions of dollars. These images of ridiculous excess and exuberance are red flags for the coming financial storm. In 1999 when tech stocks did collapse, losses reduced market capitalization by $5 billion. Some stocks fell 50% or more in a single day of trading.

Everyone is Panicking

You make your best investments when everyone is selling scared. *Millionaires are made when sellers are in a panic.* Investing virtuoso Warren Buffet refers to this as being greedy when others are fearful and fearful when others are greedy. During the global financial crisis, properties in foreclosure could be purchased for half of their 2007 pre-market peak. When we ran the numbers on houses in 2010, they were cheaper to buy than the cost of materials and labor to build them. If these types of properties are located in area with major employers and long-term population growth, they are undervalued. If the rents will cover the mortgage and monthly expenses, you are looking at an investment with minimal risk and tremendous upside potential. Being able to purchase when prices are near the bottom, and when there are fewer buyers allows investors to add significantly to their portfolios. These opportunities do not come along often, but when they do, it is time to go all in and accumulate as many assets as you can with a manageable debt load.

Consumer Credit Cycles

Consumer credit also works in cycles with periods when lending is easy and others when loan requirements become more stringent. Watch for people leveraging up on excessive consumer debt. This is usually fueled by a rapid increase in the value of their primary residence or stock portfolio. As assets appreciate, people spend this perceived wealth, which is another form of lifestyle inflation. In tandem, access to consumer credit loosens as lenders view higher asset levels as a justification to extend additional consumer credit. Be cautious if your neighbors are overspending on bigger homes, expensive cars, RVs, or boats based on the appreciation of their home or retirement portfolios; these can be the initial signs of the next downturn.

Just before the global financial crisis we saw friends being approved for million-dollar home loans with incomes that did not justify such debt. One of our wiser friends, who was approved for a $900,000 mortgage, chose to take a loan of $250,000. His comment to us, "no one knows more about my ability to repay this loan than me, and there is no way I can service a $900,000 loan." Banks across the country were taking on these massive risks in approving such loans. The situation became more dire when underwriting standards for verifying a borrower ability to repay the debt also declined. When the credit markets are over lending in this manner it usually doesn't end well for those who are overleveraged.

Government Debt

One of the more serious risks in the next two decades is excessive government debt levels and deficit spending. This is not just a risk to those in the United States, this is a global risk due to the contagion effect that occurs in other countries when the U.S. economy falters. The U.S. Congress has the power to levy taxes and spend money, which includes creating a federal budget. When creating a budget, members of Congress can compromise and cut various programs to create a balanced budget. Government then only spends what it collects in tax revenue. However, if government spending exceeds what it collects in taxes, a deficit is created. The government must rely on debt by issuing U.S. Treasuries, which we discussed in chapter 14, to cover this extra spending.

Deficit Spending

For decades the U.S. Congress has spent more than it collects from taxes and has been running deficits. *This is the government equivalent of lifestyle inflation.* According to the Congressional Budget Office, the federal government's annual deficit is just over $1 trillion in fiscal year 2019 and estimated to be $1.1 trillion by fiscal year 2020. *Let this figure sink in for a moment, the U.S. government is spending $1 trillion a year in money it does not have, and the number is rising each year at a significant pace.* Congress is acting like an intoxicated lottery winner, but with *your* money. Some economists will argue these deficits can easily be paid off as the economy expands, but we have seen tremendous economic expansion since the global financial crisis and prior to it, yet this debt burden continues to grow for future generations to contend with.

Government Debt, Get Nervous

The U.S. government holds some of this debt (Treasuries) itself such as in the Social Security Trust Fund. The government also sells debt to the public, mostly to domestic investors and various entities. It also, to a lesser extent, sells to foreign investors and foreign countries. Individuals and entities are willing to buy this debt even though it offers a low interest rate, because the debt holders believe there is a minimal risk of default. If the debt levels continue to rise in the future, both foreign and domestic buyers may be less willing to acquire U.S. government debt unless they are paid a higher interest rate.

If the U.S. government must pay a higher rate of interest on future debt, the total cost of debt servicing will rise. If you had to pay 1% more on a debt of $1 trillion you would owe $10 billion more per year in interest. That is $10 billion that is not available for social services, expanding space exploration, improving schools, or modernizing our transportation infrastructure.

However, $10 billion per year in interest is only the tip of the iceberg. The U.S. federal debt, which is the total amount of debt from running many years of annual deficits, reached $22 *trillion* in 2019. If we use a U.S. population statistic of 329 million people, this level of debt equates to nearly $67,000 for every person. *Think about that for a moment, nearly $67,000 in debt for every single person in the country. Now consider how hard it is to pay off $67,000 in debt, especially if you are piling on more debt every year.*

The U.S. Congressional Budget Office expects the national debt to increase to more than $33 trillion by 2028. That would be a 50% increase and the average citizen's share of that debt would be over $100,000. The total of all the goods and services produced by the United States is called the Gross Domestic Product (GDP). If you were to think of the United States economy as one big business, the GDP would be everything the business produces. By 2028, and possibly sooner, our national debt will be equal to our GDP, which means our debt will be equal to almost everything the U.S. economy produces in an entire year. Yet, members of Congress and more suprisingly most citizens seem unconcerned.

Bring in the Fringe

In an effort to rationalize such massive debt levels, formerly fringe economic theories are coming into fashion. These theories claim that massive deficits are not a concern as long as inflation stays low. Unfortunately, there is no such thing as a guarantee for low inflation; in chapter 14 we discussed times of high inflation and double digit interest rates in the early 1980s. These levels of inflation and high interest rates could return again which would severely increase the burden of the national debt. Personally, I believe these deficits are putting the U.S. and the global economy at tremendous risk. Accordingly, I strongly encourage you to factor this risk in to your long-term financial plans.

Plan for Higher Taxes

This lack of fiscal discipline by the U.S. Congress will have consequences that could jeopardize your financial freedom. Federal income and capital gains tax rates will likely increase. As discussed in chapter 17, expect reductions in Social Security Retirement Benefits and an increase in the Full Retirement Age from the current 67 years old. Federal Insurance Contributions Act (FICA) taxes will also likely increase, both for employers and employees to put Social Security programs on a more solid financial footing. FICA tax may be applied to more forms of income and the current wage ceiling of $137,700 for FICA taxes could be lifted to have FICA apply to all wage income.

Remaining Untaxable?

A second area of concern is that laws can change and there is no guarantee that the retirement programs we have today will retain the same benefits. In the future, tax free investments like Roth IRAs, Coverdell Education IRA Savings Accounts and 529 College Savings plans <u>may not remain tax free</u>. In January 2015 then President Barack Obama suggested eliminating the tax-free benefits of 529 college savings plans. Proposals of this nature are more likely in the coming years as the government looks for ways to help reduce the significant debt burden that exists.

Factor these potential legislative changes into your long-term financial planning. *Your financial freedom will not be durable if you don't include the possibility of higher rates across all forms of taxes in the years to come.* If I am wrong, you will be rewarded with an extra cushion of income, but if I am right you will be well prepared.

Key Takeaways:

• It is important to keep track of broader market trends. Markets work in cycles, like the Biblical story of the seven fat years and seven lean years. When things are going well, financially prepare yourself for potential bad times so you can profit when markets decline.

• There are times when irrational exuberance triumphs over rational thinking. This leads to asset bubbles and eventually rapid declines in asset values. Proper due diligence will help you avoid overpaying for assets or becoming overleveraged on credit.

• The collapse of bubbles are the times to create wealth, by buying assets at a discount. Follow Warren Buffet's advice, "be fearful when others are greedy and greedy when others are fearful."

• Governments can overindulge on debt financing and succumb to lifestyle inflation, just like consumers. The U.S. government has overindulged for decades and the current debt levels are unsustainable. This will create problems globally, not just in the United States.

• The rising debt levels in the U.S. are likely to drive tax rates higher in the future. Tax free accounts such as Roth IRAs, Education IRAs, and 529 College Savings Plans may not remain tax free. The more you understand taxes, the more you can make intelligent tax decisions, and protect yourself against future tax hikes.

CHAPTER 24: IMPROVING EFFICIENCY

Part of the process of this book is looking for ways to increase your efficiency to improve your results. Which will accelerate your progress in achieving your goals. Often adding a few habits to your daily routine to keep your mind focused on the long-term prize of financial freedom and maximizing your happiness is all it takes.

Write a Daily To-Do List

At night before going to bed keep a notebook handy to write your to-do list for the next day. Highlight the task on the list that will most advance your goal of achieving financial freedom. This highlighted task is your primary goal for tomorrow. Don't focus on the easier tasks because they provide a sense of accomplishment, focus on the meaningful task that brings tangible results.

Writing down your to-do list also gets these thoughts out of your mind to help you sleep. Interestingly while we are asleep our brain continues to solve these puzzles so often when you first wake up you will have the solution to a task on your list but you were not consciously thinking about it.

This list is your action plan for the day, stay focused on the highlighted task until it is completed. If you retain a record of these tasks in a notebook, they serve as a track record of your progress. You will see writing a daily list of tasks in Stage 6 of the *10 Stages Workbook*. I encourage you not to use your phone for this list. Your phone should not be in the same room where you sleep. Its presence will impede your sleeping. If necessary transfer the tasks you need for the day from paper to your phone.

Vocalize Your Goals

Vocalize your goals to your network of contacts, including new contacts. This approach builds off the concept that many hands make light work. If you tell people you are looking for a small commercial property in a certain part of town, you now have many other people thinking about this request. If a person comes across this type of property, they will remember you were interested in buying it.

The same approach applies if you are looking for a great plumber or for a new job in a specific sector. I once met a woman visiting from Washington D.C. at a conference in Uganda who told me she needed to hire a forestry expert for a project. She needed this person to speak Spanish and have some prior overseas experience. Turns out, I had a friend who was perfect for her project. I introduced them over email and she hired him. By vocalizing her goals to everyone she met, even while on a trip to Uganda, she found exactly what she needed.

Don't Emphasize the Negative

What we focus on in life expands to consume our time and thoughts. If you make a mistake, write down why you think this mistake occurred and the lessons you learned. The goal is to appreciate the mistake by learning from it so you can avoid making it again. Try to avoid replaying the mistake repeatedly in your head or criticizing yourself for making it. This is sometimes much harder to do than to say, but try to recognize that mistakes are a learning process.

The more you focus on what you learned, you begin to view these errors for what they are, minor educational setbacks. Making mistakes improves and sharpen your skills over time. Even major mistakes can be overcome with time and persistence. If you aren't making any mistakes you are probably not taking the calculated risks needed to expand your skills and grow.

Underselling Skills and Bias

Everyone has a certain level of skills and they may excel in certain areas such as math, writing, public speaking, or problem solving. If you see a great public speaker and think to yourself, "I can't do that," you are underselling your skills. Maybe you can't present to an audience that well today, but with practice you will become significantly better. You want to look at the progress you hope to achieve to make yourself better, don't start by comparing yourself to the end result. It may have taken years of practice for this person to be such a good public speaker.

Similarly, because this individual is a great public speaker, we may attribute other skills to them that they have not demonstrated. This is a form of bias, we assume their skill in one area translates to skill in other areas. You might assume this great presenter is also a skilled investor or technical expert or a talented manager, but in reality they may fall short on all three.

If you recognize this bias you are less likely to undersell your skills, while also acknowledging they can be improved with training and practice. This plays into efficiency because underselling your skills will prevent you from reaching your full potential. Similarly, you put yourself at risk if you overestimate someone's overall talents just because they show great skills in one area. A person great at sales may be unable to control production costs or can't follow through in filling the orders they have secured. You need to verify skills in other areas before assuming they exist or it could lead to costly mistakes.

Avoiding Distractions

The one defining factor I see that separates people who are creating wealth from those who are not, is how they spend their free time. Wealth creators are constantly seeking new knowledge and skills, they are reading books, listening to podcasts, and always hunting for their next investment. They are thinking creatively about how to reduce costs and expenses or finding ways to get what they want at a discount. They use their evenings to make progress on their goals for tomorrow.

Many people who could become wealthier don't because they spend their evenings binge watching television, going down a rabbit hole of YouTube videos, or spend hours on social media or playing video games. All these entertainment options are fine in moderation, but they can quickly rob you of your valuable free time. Set limits for yourself such as a 15 minute timer on your phone. When it goes off you are done with this distraction for the evening. As you write down what will motivate you it may help to ask yourself each night, "Do I want to update my social media or post a new picture or do I want to be a millionaire?" As you add up these nights over many years that is precisely the choice you are making.

Key Takeaways

• Keep a running list of your goals, review them before you go to bed and highlight the most important goal for the following day. That is your target when you wake up.

• Vocalize your goals to other people who will help you on your quest. Many hands make light work.

• Don't overemphasize the negative, find a process that helps you accept and learn from your mistakes. This is easier said than done, but it will help you move past mistakes instead of being constrained by them.

• Be careful of bias when it comes to underselling your skills or overestimating the skills of others. Your skills can improve with practice and training. Don't assume a person's talents in one area translate to skills in another; this can lead to costly mistakes.

• Be productive with your free time and look to increase your knowledge and skills. Avoid spending too much time on unproductive distractions, such as television, videos and social media.

CHAPTER 25: PURSUIT OF HAPPINESS

Wealth alone will not get you to where you need to be, you must also focus on improving aspects of your life that will make you happy. This chapter includes strategies for keeping your mental wellbeing at the forefront of your daily actions. There are also suggestions on how to process the challenges you will face along the way.

Control, Influence, Appreciate

One of the best pieces of advice I was given in college was by a fantastic political science professor who said, "In life you will be happier if you can recognize that there are things you can control, things you can influence, and things you can merely appreciate." As you face a challenge take a moment to analyze the issue and decide in which of these three categories it belongs. If it is a challenge that is under your direct control, then resolve it. If you can influence it, find the channels to exert the pressure needed for change. However, there are going to be challenges that, at least in the short term, you can merely appreciate.

You are not going to revise major legislation or change your entire financial situation overnight, so don't expend energy becoming angry or frustrated about it. Channel this energy into specific activities that will create influence. If the issue is related to legislation, your influence could involve fundraising, volunteering your time, or meeting with elected officials. Take productive steps towards influencing the change you wish to see; simply complaining or being angry does nothing. This matches the famous quote by Mahatma Gandhi, "*You must be the change you wish to see in the world.*"

Poisoning Our Future

I would be remiss if I did not raise two worrying trends over the last decade. The first is the increasing self-selection of news and information by people to reinforce existing opinions. This approach to information will not make you wiser or help you understand the value of compromise and negotiation, regardless of where you fall on the ideological/political spectrum. Sealing yourself off from different points of view is fueling the tribalism that may become a systemic threat to the future of your country. Having spent time in countries undergoing civil wars and social upheaval I have seen firsthand how these trends emerge slowly, seeming only minor at first, but then cascade with devastating results.

To counter this trend, turn off the politicized news and stop reading and forwarding stories or articles that make you feel outraged or like a victim. For some the dopamine high from this information becomes an addiction. This habit is detrimental to your physical health and mental wellbeing and won't help you advance towards your long-term goals. In fact, it will hold you back and inhibit your success.

If you want to make a difference and feel empowered, identify any one of the genuine issues facing our society, the rampant prescription drug dependency, income inequality, the dangerous federal debt levels, social inequality, racism, environmental degradation, and the decline of jobs that offer a living wage, and take steps to make positive change. This replaces the vicious cycle of tribalism with the virtuous cycle of contributing to positive change.

Work/Life Balance

In recent decades workers are working more hours per week which correlates to higher stress levels on both individuals and families. The notion of a work/life balance is replaced with employees always being available to employers. Responding to email at all hours, staying at work until late, going in early and traveling on the weekends encroaches on time that was allotted for friends and family. It is remarkable how many people just accept this as the norm. It is unsurprising to see the breakdown of communication within our communities described given that so many of us are stressed to a breaking point and overly focused on work.

A poor work/life balance deprives us of the time we need to recharge in order to perform at our best. It also hinders us from attending our kids' sporting events or school plays, missing out on time with friends and neglecting hobbies that provide us with joy. Everyone needs relaxing activities to center themselves. Neglecting your work/life balance will take a toll on your health and wellbeing. As you define your specific goals be sure that they include strategies to address a healthy work/life balance. You can redline your mind and body for short periods, but high stress levels for a sustained period will begin to take a serious toll on your physical and mental health.

Balance May Only Cost $2 Per Hour

People are sometimes striving to quit their jobs to get the freedom they desire, but the answer could be as simple as switching to a position with less responsibility. For example, I have a friend who I will call Dean, who was looking at two jobs offers. The first was to be a divisional manager that was slightly higher than his current position. Another position was as a deputy divisional manager, which paid about $6 less per hour in gross income. Dean went through the process of figuring out his actual per hour earnings as explained in chapter 6.

Dean discovered the difference between the two jobs was only $2 per hour after deducting for higher taxes and the expected additional hours worked. Dean asked himself if it was worth $2 per hour to take the higher level job and all the extra stress that came with the position. Giving up $2 per hour would give him a much healthier work/life balance and allow him to spend more time with his family and to exercise regularly. The allocation of your time and your sense of happiness are intertwined. Don't give away happiness for $2 per hour.

Be Confident, But Humble

We will never experience a shortage of blowhards and ego-maniacs in the world. We seem to create them at a remarkably sustainable rate. They are usually painful to listen to and never a person you seek out for advice. Trying to avoid being one of these people is a good reminder when discussing your successes or achievements. If it is perceived as arrogance you are more likely to create resentment instead of positive relationships.

There is value in being confident, but humble. Sometimes the smartest person in the room is the one who has yet to say a word. You want to be humble to get others to share their honest ideas. Also, don't start forming your next question in your head when you should be listening. This may cause you to miss key information such as the reveal we discussed in chapter 22. Be confident, but always view your skills in an objective manner, as hubris frequently leads to mistakes.

One incident always comes to my mind when I think about the importance of combining confidence with humility. Probably the smartest person I have ever met was a guy named Andy who sadly died young of pancreatic cancer. We met in late 2003 and became quick friends. In 2004 I mentioned I was selling an apartment because I thought real estate was becoming over-valued and prices may soon fall. In Andy's characteristically understated way, he said, "let's grab a beer, I have a few thoughts on that topic." I jumped on the offer and while we sat at bar in northern Virginia, he explained on a cocktail napkin how we were heading into a terrible financial crisis. He said it would be the closest thing we have seen to the Great Depression of the

1930s. Andy described the rapid overleveraging occurring in investment banking and the growing risks of collateralized debt related to housing and commercial real estate. He said loans are given that should never be approved and the level of defaults would soon be massive.

Andy explained how complex and highly leveraged these financial instruments had become and how the banks were all entangled in a financial web and it would be hard to unwind these assets. He said that once credit starts to seize, the finance sector is going to grind to a halt, banks are going to collapse, and the crisis will become global. I was floored by what he said. At the time I was expecting a notable decline in real estate prices, but not massive contagion throughout the global economy. This was about three years before the global financial crisis ensued and his prediction played out exactly as described. When Andy made his prediction virtually all the financial commentators were bullish on the future of the economy, and he was the only one I heard make such a dire and accurate prediction.

When the financial crisis began to unfold, I called him to say, "Andy, you called it, the news says no one could have seen this coming, but you laid out this whole scenario years ago." He gave a slight laugh and said, "yeah, you win some, you lose some." Andy had made the greatest financial predictions I have ever seen, besting scores of famous economists and business leaders, and his response was pure modesty. I often think of Andy and his example of confidence and humility, and it reminds me how truly remarkable he was as a person.

Strength from Struggling

Overcoming challenges and fighting to succeed is a process that teaches us resilience and persistence. Embrace these periods of struggle and recognize that they shape us to be more durable and resourceful. In chapter 18 I relayed my experience working in a family sign business and the valuable lessons it provided.

However, what I left out was that this time soon came to a sad end. My dad tragically passed away when I was 17 and my brother and I had to close the business we started together. The emotional loss was numbing, and in the months that followed I switched to working full-time at a car dealership while completing high school. These were exhausting 14-hour days but the process, as hard as it was, brought strength and resilience.

Most successful entrepreneurs have failed or declared bankruptcy along the way, but they pulled themselves back up and started climbing again. None of them will say it was easy. But you never read about the ones who give up and stop climbing. I respect that many people in this world have been dealt a difficult hand and many have experienced all the heartache and struggle they need for generations, but I believe there is tremendous strength to be gained from these struggles if you can channel it into tenacity to achieve your goals.

Grit and Gratitude

Grit is what helps us to overcome the struggles we face, but the other necessary component is gratitude. Be grateful for the talents and opportunities you have been given; there are many others who would give anything to be in your position. If you need a strong lesson in gratitude, volunteer in a low income community or a developing country, or take time off from work to join in the recovery efforts after a natural disaster. It will immediately put your life into perspective. Take time to appreciate your successes as they happen, instead of immediately chasing the next conquest. Take some time every day to calm your mind, meditate, and reflect on your blessings, as it will help keep life in perspective and support your goals of maximizing happiness.

Everyone Faces Self-Doubt

The impression of the overnight success or the perennially confident business superstar or athlete is mostly a myth. People regularly wrestle with self-doubt and uncertainty along the way. They question their talents or their ideas and at times they even feel like a fraud for not being a better version of themselves. This is human nature so try to surround yourself with supportive people who lift you up when you are down by creating a positive and productive atmosphere. Try not to put too much pressure on yourself, although this is often much harder than we are all willing to accept. There are always new opportunities around the corner and ways to overcome the challenges of today. Recognize that self-doubt is normal, but don't let it hinder your focus or progress towards financial freedom and happiness in life.

Marriage and Life Partners

No single decision will impact your future quality of life than whom you choose to marry or with whom you choose to spend your life. The type of person might change significantly as you age and learn from life's experiences, so its not a decision to rush. You and your partner need to be aligned on your philosophy about money. Half of divorces are related to money as are a considerable number of marital arguments. If you remove money as a source of tension in your relationship, you have preempted a lifetime of arguments. It is tremendously helpful to work through these money discussions well before you make a lifelong commitment.

75%/25% Salary Split

Perhaps you are thinking that last paragraph is nice advice, but a little too late. You are already in a committed relationship and although you two love each other you are not on the same page about money. In situations when one partner is frugal, and the other is a spender you must come together to agree on a plan.

One tool we used when we first got married was to split our income. We put 75% of our respective incomes in a joint bank account and the remaining 25% in personal accounts. It does not matter who makes a higher salary, 75% goes into the joint account. The joint account pays for all monthly bills related to core necessities. This includes housing, utilities, basic transportation, groceries, joint travel or vacations, and student loan payments. For certain expenses, set a ceiling such as $300 per month for a vehicle payment or $200 for clothes; anything above this ceiling comes out of that person's personal account.

The money in your 25% personal accounts is free to spend as you choose. A few key categories that fall within the 25% account are eating out, entertainment, any luxury items, solo travel or vacations, gifts for each other and any expenditures above the ceilings that have been set. Although we started our relationship using this 75%/25% split we soon found we no longer needed it and merged our accounts. But it was a valuable tool to get us to a shared understanding of how we would manage our money.

Keep Your Backs Together

A marriage or any long-term partnership is about putting your backs together. You must be focused on each other's needs and never trying to identify how much "more" you are giving. A partnership is not about keeping score. When it comes to personal relationships once you feel like you have given everything you can give, then give 10% more and you are probably where you need to be.

The focus can't be about one individual, the priority is always on each other and your children. A good sense of humor and listening more than you talk goes a long way in helping to keep your backs together. It also helps to clarify prior to starting a discussion if the other party is just listening or being asked for advice to fix a problem. This helps to make sure you are both on the same page *before* you launch into a topic.

Adequate Sleep

As part of your tasks in Stage 3 of your workbook you will set an early bedtime to provide a healthy sleep cycle. Adequate sleep is proven to be critical to your long-term health and daily cognitive functions. Fortunately, the days of people claiming they can perform at the highest levels while only sleeping a few hours a night appear to be over. Going to bed at the same time every night prepares your mind for a rhythm of sleeping which is crucial to your long-term success. If I am off my sleep cycle for a few days because of traveling I can instantly feel its impact on my productivity and cognitive abilities. Once you have established this sleep cycle and made it an integral habit you will be very reluctant to give it up.

As Old as Your Spine and Knees

Being healthy and physically fit bolsters your sense of happiness as well as your finances by lowering health related expenses. Accordingly, that is why a few of your tasks in the *10 Stages Workbook* are about going for walks at lunch to recharge, taking yoga classes and adding a regular exercise regime to your weekly schedule.

If you walk to work you are getting exercise and eliminating your need for a car, thus lowering transportation expenses. Factoring physical fitness into your housing, transportation, food and entertainment decisions can promote long term health and reduce expenses. Studies by the Mayo Clinic show High Intensity Interval Training (HIIT) classes are the best type of exercise at any age, but especially for older people or those who are trying to get back in shape. The feeling of indestructible youth starts to fade in your 30s, but you are only as old as your spine and knees. If you take care of yourself, curb your stress levels, and stay fit and active, you can continue to tick off your goals in life.

One common theme emphasized in this book is the need to prepare for future health care costs which continue to climb. We referenced the 2019 Fidelity Investments study that shows a retiring 65-year-old couple needs about $285,000 to cover health care and medical expenses throughout their retirement. This figure is a 78% increase of Fidelity Investment's 2002 estimate of $160,000. *Health costs will likely continue to rise in the coming years and individuals seeking to retire well below the age of 65 must have income streams to cover these costs.*

In 2018 Fidelity polled 1,000 people between 50 and 64 who retired in the past three years. They found that although almost all these early retirees had some form of health insurance, 36% were paying $500 a month or more in health care premiums. A healthy diet and a regime of regular exercise is a way to improve your odds of being healthy and may serve you well in lowering your future health expenses. Creating wealth and promoting happiness truly requires a systemic approach which includes sleep and exercise. These are not steps that you can skip if you want to maximize your efficiency in achieving your goals.

Key Takeaways

• Recognize in life there are things you can control, things you can influence and things you can only accept and appreciate. Responding to each of these in the right way will help to manage your stress levels.

• Avoid the negativity, particularly on social media, that permeates modern politics and social issues. These are distractions from what is important in life.

• A healthy work/life balance may only cost a few dollars an hour in a lower salary, so look at options that may reduce your salary slightly but will provide you the time you are seeking for other aspects of life.

• Struggles may be painful, but they can be the foundation for building strength and grit that converts into future success. Be grateful for what you have and appreciate each stage in life.

• Be confident and humble, as it helps build positive relationships and is the best way to draw out the smartest people around you. Also recognize that periods of self-doubt are common even in the greatest champions.

• Fights about money will harm your personal relationships. You must communicate with your spouse or significant other to become aligned on your long-term plans with money. Try using the 75% joint account and 25% personal account split for all income. And remember to always keep your backs together.

• Adequate sleep and exercise are crucial to long-term happiness and lowering future health care costs.

CHAPTER 26: RETIREMENT STRESS TEST

Before you embark on early retirement, put your plan through a few stress tests to assess its financial durability and your emotional response to quitting full-time work. In Stage 9 of the *10 Stages Workbook* there is a specific task to help you run a financial stress test on your investments to protect against potential downside risks. These include a significant loss in your stock portfolio or an unusually high number of vacancies in your rental properties due to losing a major employer in the area. This task will help you assess and mitigate risk and improve the durability of your financial plan.

The act of retiring early can be emotionally unsettling for some, so your first test is to see how you react to this sudden decline in income. You can soften the blow by easing into retirement. If you are a couple, one person could quit their job first to experience living on one income. This will help you determine whether adjustments are needed before you both quit. If you are single, switch to part-time employment for six months or a year before quitting completely. You could also look to line up consulting work one or two days a week, just to keep connected to former colleagues and to bring in some income.

Most people feel their career is part of their identity and their job provides many of their daily social connections. This leads to the second stress test. You need to determine how leaving your job will affect you emotionally and how it will change your social circle. Some workers have more of their identity invested in their jobs than they realize. Beyond the income it provides, jobs provide a sense of status, empowerment, or makes people feel like a productive member of the society.

A period of leave without pay or taking a long block of leave will help you navigate how emotionally tied you are to your job and the status it affords. Consider options for working part-time, entrepreneurial ventures or volunteering to replace the social connections you will lose. Retirees sometimes only plan for what they want to do in the first few months of retirement. You really need to have plans for the first few years of retirement. You want to be moving towards something positive, not just leaving your job.

But, remember this book is about giving you options to retire early but that may not be one of your goals. You can always keep working full-time if you enjoy it, while knowing financially you can quit at any time.

Define Your Day

As you near retirement you need to think through how you will spend these unfilled hours each day. The absence of a plan can lead to boredom and depression. In addition, early retirees sometimes forget that most of their friends will still be working. You need to have a plan to fill these hours. Retirement expert Wes Moss suggests early retirees have at least three core pursuits. These include three specific endeavors or activities that will provide them with enjoyment.

His research also suggests that happier retirees volunteer regularly and don't spend an excessive amount of time on solitary activities like reading alone, fishing alone, or hunting alone. Moss also finds that happier retirees take two and half vacations per year, spend more on each vacation and vacation for a longer period. These are a few factors to consider as you map out how you will spend your time in retirement.

Mini-Retirements During a Career

One way to prepare for retirement is try it out a few times during your career with mini-retirements. You might work for five years and then take a year off to explore other interests or travel. This is an excellent way to avoid becoming burned out from working. You can also test out how you feel both financially and socially when you are no longer tied to a job. These breaks will allow you to enjoy some large blocks of free time at different stages of your life, instead of waiting until the end of your career. If you have a positive track record with your current employer, they may let you leave and come back. As mentioned before anything is open to negotiation if you take the time to come up with a plan and are flexible in your options.

Major Expenses Before You Retire

Make all your major purchases prior to walking away from full-time employment. These can be personal expenses like getting that sports car you always wanted, setting aside funds to pay for your kids' college, or hiring Iron Maiden to play your retirement party.

You may also want to complete capital improvements on your rental properties. If you use your job income to fund new roofs, upgraded appliances and painting properties you will retire with significantly more reserves for capital expenses. Completing these tasks in advance provides an extra cushion in your financial plan and you won't have to spend your early retirement running through a list of renovations and repairs.

Testing Out Living Overseas

As mentioned in chapter 13 it can be both exciting and cost effective to spend part of the year living abroad during retirement. Overseas life is not for everyone, but it does provide a chance to move away from cold winters while taking advantage of new experiences. There is much truth to the phrase you rest, you rust. Mapping out a plan to live abroad regularly or periodically also can provide the extended vacations that can be helpful for mental wellbeing in retirement. In addition, it can help cut down on your annual expenses as you rent your current home while living in a country with a lower cost of living. If you choose to change the country you visit each year and can provide a great way to slowly see the world during retirement and truly dig into the history, food, and culture of other countries. Be sure to do your research and due diligence before you travel and make sure your travel documents and travel insurance are all up to date before you depart.

Protect Yourself from Fraud

It is a sad fact of life that the elderly often become targets of financial predators. Bloomberg reports that seniors may lose $36.5 billion a year, with other studies saying this figure is "grossly underestimated" as most cases are not reported to authorities. A 2014 study found that in nearly 60 percent of cases the perpetrator was a family member. Part of your responsibility for financial independence is creating systems that will protect you against being a victim of financial exploitation both from strangers and family members.

As you age your ability to protect yourself may decline, so build durable protections as soon as you retire. Some measures to consider are providing read only access to banking details to a trusted family member to help monitor your finances. Or plan to reduce the complexity of your investments if necessary. We covered annuities as a simple investment option to provide a regular income stream. Take an honest look at your family history regarding early onset dementia or similar health issues to assess your risk levels and have people who can help you if your cognitive abilities begin to diminish.

Key Takeaways

• Stress test your retirement by taking an extended period off from work, both to experience living on a lower income level and to determine how psychologically and emotionally you are tied to the structure and status of your job.

• Consider a career with multiple mini-retirements to provide large blocks of time to pursue other interests. Working for a few years and then taking a year off is a great way to enjoy part of your retirement when you are younger and will help you to return to work recharged.

• Pay off any major expenses and make any major purchases before you retire. You don't want to incur these expenses after you quit work working.

• Define how you will spend your days in retirement; have at least three activities or hobbies to focus on with your time.

• Consider spending part of the year living abroad in retirement it is a great way to stay active and may save you money.

• Protect yourself from fraud before you become older by creating mechanisms that will simplify your investments and protect your income streams.

Start the Become Loaded for Life! 10 Stages Workbook

If you have made it this far in the book and have yet to get a copy of the *Become Loaded for Life! 10 Stages Workbook* now is the time. The workbook is the practical step-by-step guide to turning your dreams of financial freedom into a reality, while also seeking to maximize your happiness in life. As you work through each of the ten stages you will see your progress unfold. Get started, stay focused and make your luck!

APPENDIX 1:

1. <u>Accredited Investors:</u> Initially crowd funding investment platforms were restricted to accredited investors. According to the U.S. Securities and Exchange Commission (SEC), for an individual to be considered an accredited investor, they must have a minimum net worth of $1 million, excluding the value of their primary residence, or have annual income of at least $200,000 each year for the last two years, or if married, $300,000 in joint income for the last two years. There also must be an expectation that the investor will continue to make this income level in the current year. In the wake of the financial crisis the government is trying to protect less experienced investors from early stage investments which are higher risk and speculative in nature.

<u>Non Accredited Investors</u>: There has been some loosening of this rule for crowd funding investments. The SEC approved Title III of the JOBS Act, referred to as the Crowdfunding Act, and now any investor is able to invest in securities from registered crowdfunding platforms, but there are restrictions on the amount that can be invested based on income levels. Details were provided in a SEC Investor Bulletin released on May 10, 2017.

The table below taken from the SEC Investor Bulletin provides examples of investment levels:

Annual Income	Net Worth	Calculation	12-month Limit
$30,000	$105,000	greater of $2,200 or 5% of $30,000 ($1,500)	$2,200
$150,000	$80,000	greater of $2,200	$4,000

		or 5% of $80,000 ($4,000)	
$150,000	$107,000	10% of $107,000 ($10,000)	$10,700
$200,000	$900,000	10% of $200,000 ($20,000)	$20,000
$1.2 million	$2 million	10% of $1.2 million ($120,000), subject to cap	$107,000

In regard to calculating net worth for crowdfunding investments, an investor does not include their primary residence among their assets when making the calculation, but a spouse's income and assets can be combined. For a couple, their combined crowdfunding investments cannot exceed the limit that would apply to an individual investor at that annual income or net worth level. Using the chart above, a married couple with a combined annual income of $150,000 and a net worth of $80,000 would be limited to investing $4,000 in a 12-month period.

Legislation and regulations related to investing in securities on crowdfunding platforms are still evolving as it remains a relatively new field of investing. Similarly, the number of investment platforms that exist is fluid as new firms emerge. Online searches for crowdfunding and peer to peer lending will provide lists of current platforms. Also, be sure to conduct your proper due diligence on firms by looking at online reviews before you provide them with your personal information or invest money.

2.Grid of Exceptions to 10% Early Withdrawal Penalty for Tax Deferred Retirement Accounts.

The distribution will not be subject to the 10%	Exception to 10% Additional Tax

early distribution penalty tax in the following circumstances:	Qualified Plans 401(k) etc.	IRA, SEP, Plans	Internal Revenue Code Section or Reference
Age			
After participant/IRA owner reaches age 59½	Yes	Yes	72(t)(2)(A)(i)
Rule 55: After being fired, laid off or quitting			
Participant is between ages of 55 - 59½ and was fired, laid off, or quit their job. Participant is limited to withdrawing from their 401(k) plan with this most recent employer	Yes	No	See Topic Number 558 - Additional Tax on Early Distributions from Retirement Plans Other Than IRAs
Death			
After death of the participant/IRA owner	Yes	Yes	72(t)(2)(A)(ii)
Disability			
Total and permanent disability of the participant/IRA owner	Yes	Yes	72(t)(2)(A)(iii)
Education			
Qualified higher education expenses	No	Yes	72(t)(2)(E)
Equal Payments (SSEP)			
Series of substantially equal payments	Yes	Yes	72(t)(2)(A)(iv)
First time Homebuyers			
Qualified first-time homebuyers, up to $10,000	No	Yes	72(t)(2)(F)
Unreimbursed Medical Expenses/Insurance			
Amount of unreimbursed medical expenses (> 7.5% AGI; after 2012, 10% if under age 65)	Yes	Yes	72(t)(2)(B)
Health insurance premiums paid while unemployed	No	Yes	72(t)(2)(D)
Military Reservists Called to Active Duty			

Certain distributions to qualified military reservists called to active duty	Yes	Yes	72(t)(2)(G)
Roth Rollovers			
In-plan Roth rollovers or eligible distributions contributed to another retirement plan or IRA within 60 days (also see FAQs: Waivers of the 60-Day Rollover Requirement)	Yes	Yes	402(c), 402A(d)(3), 403(a)(4), 403(b)(8), 408(d)(3), 408A(d)(3)
Separation from Government Service			
The employee separates from service during or after the year the employee reaches age 55 (age 50 for public safety employees of a state, or political subdivision of a state, in a governmental defined benefit plan)	Yes	No	72(t)(2)(A)(v), 72(t)(10)

APPENDIX 2:

Below is a condensed list of the 70 tasks in the *Become Loaded for Life! 10 Stages Workbook.* To truly understand the process behind these tasks please read the full workbook which includes detailed explanations for each task. The context will help you implement each task.

Introduction
- Write the five key long-term goals of what you want your life to look like in five to seven years.
- Write down five skills, experiences or places that you will obtain, complete, or visit as part of this process. You will add a new one each time you complete an item on the list.
- Write down your real hourly rate of income after deducting for taxes, your extra commuting time and any other necessary reductions. Also write down the real hourly rate for another job you would really like to do.
- Begin tracking all your monthly expenses starting today and track your expenses over the past year.

Stage 1
1. I have written my first financial independence and wellbeing plan _____ Done!
2. I am tracking my spending and budgeting and have identified three negative spending patterns I have changed. _____ Done!
3. I have saved $250 in my Emergency Fund and I am depositing $50 per week into this account. _____ Done!
4. I have not eaten at a restaurant for three weeks and bought everything I ate from a grocery store. _____ Done!
5. I have made a list of all my assets. I have also made a list of all my debts, who I owe, and the interest rate on each amount of debt. I have calculated my net worth and I will continue to do so on a regular basis either monthly or twice a year. _____ Done!
6. I have enrolled in my employer retirement account and I

am contributing enough to get the full employer match. _____ Done!

7. I have completed the steps of reviewing my credit report and identifying how I will resolve any blemishes. I will pay every bill on time in the future. _____ Done!

Stage 2

8. I have not used my car for three weeks and found alternative options to reduce my transportation expenses. _____ Done!

9. I have avoided lifestyle inflation and channeled all raises, bonuses and salary increases into paying off debt or into investments. _____ Done!

10. I have locked away all my credit cards, kept $50 for emergencies and I am only using a debit card. _____ Done!

11. I have an appropriate level of term life insurance and made a clear plan for when I will either increase or decrease my coverage in the future. _____ Done!

12. I have investigated options for changing where I live to significantly reduce my monthly living expenses. _____ Done!

13. I have started a constructive line of communication with my partner, so we are both on a plan for securing our financial independence. _____ Done!

14. I am walking two days a week during my lunch break, and I am looking to add more walks per week. _____ Done!

Stage 3

15. I have cleaned out my closets, garage, basement and storage units. The items were sold, donated or recycled and the money totaling $_____ has been added to my emergency fund or used to pay down debt. _____ Done!

16. I have tried several yoga classes and I have found one that I will attend at least once, if not twice, a week. _____ Done!

17. I have stuck to a set bedtime for three weeks and I will use a set bedtime that is best for my schedule to get at least eight hours of sleep. _____ Done!

18. I have stopped drinking soft drinks to improve my long-term health. _____ Done!

19. My expected annual Social Security Retirement Benefits or other forms of government superannuation program will be

$_____ per year. Starting when I am _____ years old. If I add in a 15% reduction and increase the retirement age by two years my benefit will be $_____ and my retirement age will be _____. _____ Done!

20. I have set up an account to specifically begin saving for my health care needs. This may be a traditional investment account, a Health Savings Account or a Flexible Spending Account. _____ Done!

21. I opened my Roth IRA account (or local equivalent) and made my contribution. I will seek to hit the maximum for the year and every year afterwards. _____ Done!

Stage 4

22. I have lowered my transportation expenses through public transportation, biking, or walking to work. If I must own a car it is used and economical. After completing this task my monthly expenses are now $_____ and I am saving $_____ per month. _____ Done!

23. I am spending at least 30 minutes every day on self-education. _____ Done!

24. I am taking the time to think about offers or invitations that are extended to me and I am saying no to unproductive offers. _____ Done!

25. I have found and tried ten new low-cost entertainment options as a way to lower my entertainment expenses, while also expanding my social life. _____ Done!

26. I am continuing to improve my credit by keeping small regular payments on my oldest credit cards, closing newer accounts with a zero balance and increasing my credit limit on remaining accounts. I will continue to pay off all these accounts each month and never carry a balance or pay interest on credit cards. Improving my credit will save me tens of thousands of dollars over the years from lower interest rates. _____ Done!

27. I am bringing my lunch to work; I have limited eating out to twice a month and I reduced my overall food costs by $_____ per month. _____ Done!

28.The Fix_____.
I have written down one aspect of my life that needs fixing and I am actively working on a plan to take control of this issue to prevent it from ever holding me back. _____Done!

<u>Stage 5</u>
29. I have grown my emergency fund from $5,000 to $_____ which is my *Basic Living Expenses Budget* for six months. _____ Done!

30. I have identified the people in my life who are negative and do not want what is best for me. I have taken the steps in my life to disconnect from them. I am focusing on strengthening my friendships with people who are supportive and who I will support to achieve their goals. _____ Done!

31. I have analyzed my future college savings needs and determined that I need to save $_____ to cover these expenses. Using what I have learned about investing and wealth creation I am implementing a strategy to save this amount in time for when it is needed. _____. Done!

32. I have chosen a reward and have put into place a rewards account to pay for it. I am training my brain that implementing my financial plan leads to achieving my dreams. I have spent the money and experienced the reward below. I will write down the next reward I will achieve.
Reward_____ Done!

33. I ran the numbers on 50 properties using what I learned in chapter 20 and I can identify when a property might be selling for below market prices or if there are ways to add value to the property to earn a higher rent. _____ Done!

34. I do what I say I will do; I keep my commitments. _____ Done!

35. I am now exercising three times a week in combination with walking, yoga and limiting alcohol to keep me on schedule. _____ Done!

<u>Stage 6:</u>

36. I have permanently lowered my housing expenses through some combination of roommates, buying a property, relocating or some other creative solution. I have reduced my monthly housing expenses by $_____ each month. _____ Done!

37. I have attended ten real estate meet ups in my area, and I have a list of names of investors, realtors, lenders, property managers, contractors and potential future partners. _____ Done!

38. The Fix_____. _____ Done!

39. Each night I write down my goals for the next day and I highlight the one that is the most important for achieving my long-term goals. _____ Done!

40. I have reduced my monthly expenses by $_____ and am converting $_____ to savings each month. My overall savings rate of my after-tax income is _____%. _____ Done!

<u>Stage 7:</u>

41. I have created a Lifebook and will update it on an annual basis. A trusted family member has access to it or a copy of the Lifebook. _____ Done!

42. I have a written strategy that I will review each year to balance my job risk with my portfolio risk to protect my income streams. _____ Done!

43. Every day I take a few moments to reflect on what I am grateful for in my life and realize that what I have is enough for what I truly need. _____ Done!

44. I will not fall into the trap of overvaluing promotions in my day job. I have calculated the value of a promotion at work and compared this potential reward to options to create income outside of work through investments or entrepreneurial activities. I am looking for ways to create investment opportunities that will provide a return that is equal to a promotion at various stages of the investment from negotiation, to creating value, to building equity and generating cash flow. This is the

way to create a durable exit strategy. _____ Done!

45. I have made a list of the aspects of my job that I like and dislike most. I have talked with friends about potential ideas for other jobs and listened to their feedback. I have investigated three different jobs or careers I might prefer more than my current job. I have listed the estimated hourly rate for these jobs, factoring in any reduction in my current expenses that these new jobs will bring. The three jobs and the estimated hourly rates are listed below:

Job _____ Hourly Rate _____
Job _____ Hourly Rate _____
Job _____ Hourly Rate _____
_____ Done!

46. At work I am finding ways to create value for my employer, but I am also making sure that I am not being taken advantage of by working an excessive number of hours. However, I am not obsessing about the clock and every hour I spend at work. I am saying no to unproductive offers at work in order to allocate my time and talents to create the most value for my employer. I seek to be viewed as an easy person to work with and although I am not going to be an employee forever, I am doing my best to create value for my employer while I am here. _____ Done!

47. I decided that I wanted to acquire _____ and I developed a side hustle that earned $2,000 to buy it. _____ Done!

48. I have conducted research to find ways to reduce my childcare expenses. After implementing a few strategies, I have reduced my childcare expenses by $_____ per month. _____ Done!

49. My income stream from investments and entrepreneurial activities now covers my *Basic Living Expenses Budget.*_____ Done!

Stage 8:

50. I have purchased my first investment property and I am building a real estate portfolio. _____ Done!

51. Understanding taxes is a key aspect of wealth creation. I have read two books on various aspects of taxes. I have also signed up for training or a part-time tax preparer position to learn more about taxes. _____ Done!

52. I have read the 13 Steps to Investing Foolishly from The Motley Fool. _____ Done!

53. Today I am making a conscious decision to move on from _____; it will no longer consume my thoughts. I am stronger after this event and I am ready to move past it. _____ Done!

54. I have purchased my first real estate note _____ Done!

55. I have $2,000 and the four necessary expenses (repairs, property management, vacancies and capital expenses) deducted from my monthly rents for each rental property I own. I will also look to complete any major repairs or deferred maintenance on my properties before I quit my day job and retire. _____ Done!

56. I have rewarded myself for my financial discipline by securing a credit card with rewards to help reduce the costs of future travel, experiences, or purchases. I will never carry a monthly balance on any of these cards because it would negate the benefits of these rewards. _____ Done!

Stage 9:

57. I have done a comprehensive stress test of my investment portfolio against various forms of downside risk and I have designed a strategy that will help protect against these risks if they were to occur. _____ Done!

58. I have taken all my vacation time this year and I will do the same every year going forward. _____ Done!

59. In addition to my health expenses savings account from task 20 I have purchased a rental property specifically to provide for my long-term health expenses when I am in my senior years. _____ Done!

60. I have assessed my needs for umbrella insurance and purchased a policy that will adequately protect my assets.

_____ Done!

61. For the past year I/we have lived on 50% or less of our total income. _____ Done!

62. I set aside the funds and completed lessons in _____ as a skill that I wanted to learn. Now I will write down a new skill to work towards. _____ Done!

63. I have taken a trip overseas and explored a new country and I did it without a pre-planned itinerary. _____ Done!

Stage 10:

64. I have purchased my retirement home now and will have tenants pay it off over the next 15 to 20 years. This will also allow me to eventually sell my primary residence and convert the proceeds to Immediate Income. _____ Done!

65. I have found a side hustle I enjoy doing that provides $6,000 per year. _____ Done!

66. I/We have taken a minimum of three months off (six months or a year is preferable) as a stress test of our retirement and we kept detailed notes which has taught us how to revise our future retirement goals. _____ Done!

67. I have learned how to set a credit freeze (not a credit lock or credit monitoring) to protect my credit from fraud. _____ Done!

68. I have funded all the major expenses that are necessary before I retire. _____ Done!

69. My income from investments and entrepreneurial activities are funding my *Lifestyle Expenses Budget* and I have reached financial freedom. _____ Done!

70. I am committed to helping other people who are just starting out on the path I have completed. I have made a list of all the people who have helped me on this journey, and I have provided them with something that shows my appreciation. _____ Done!

DISCLAIMER:

This book contains information and opinions and is neither personal tax advice nor legal advice. The material does not guarantee any success or profits related to your personal finances. Please consult an attorney or a tax professional for any specific tax or legal questions. Readers are advised to perform their own due diligence when it comes to investments, taxes, and financial or business decisions. All information and material that has been provided should be independently verified by your own qualified professional. No part of this publication shall be reproduced, transmitted or sold in whole or in part in any form, without the prior written consent of the author. All trademarks and registered trademarks appearing in this publication are the property of their respective owners.

ACKNOWLEDGEMENTS:

On a random afternoon I started writing some notes of financial advice for our two sons and my nephews. The pages kept coming and I quickly realized I was writing the book I wish someone had given me when I was 16 years old. I wanted to help them avoid financial mistakes, while providing a clear path for achieving financial freedom. I also wanted to help them challenge conventional wisdom, be smart with their money, and maximize their happiness.

My friends and family have been gracious through the process of writing and editing. I want to thank Matthew May, Charlie Ahmad, Annabelle and Gen Numaguchi and my wife Sarah, for their edits and constructive feedback. Our boys were also very patient when writing sometimes consumed more of our weekends than intended.

Over the years I have been fortunate to have some great mentors in my life, starting with my parents and siblings as well as great teachers and professors. When I was a far from stellar elementary school student my teacher Mr. Romano told me, "Nate, don't ever let life take away your sense of humor, because it will serve you well forever," truly great advice. Dr. Hunt at Illinois State University was tremendously generous with his time and guidance which led me to join the Peace Corps. Also thanks to Jeff N. and Dave H., fellow Illinois State students, for countless great discussions on global affairs. Over the years I have also received valuable advice from friends, particularly Brad Kath and Andy Witherspoon. I have shared some of their lessons in these pages. Most of all I want to thank Sarah, for her continuous support and for making sure we always keep our backs together.

ABOUT THE AUTHOR:

Nate Carter grew up in Chicago and became interested in personal finance at an early age. In his mid-20s he wrote a plan that turned $1,500 and a $24,000 job into financial independence in 12 years. His experience ranges from starting small businesses and co-founding a real estate company to investing in early stage start-ups and crowdfunded ventures. He is a former Peace Corps Volunteer (Morocco) and U.S. Foreign Service Officer (diplomat). He has lived and worked overseas for nearly 20 years, traveling to more than 70 countries. He holds a Masters' degree in political science and a law degree. He and his family enjoy hiking and outdoor activities. He can be found at www.loadedforlife.com.

Notes:

Introduction:

1. Less than $1,000: https://www.gobankingrates.com/saving-money/half-americans-less-savings-2017/

2. $16,000 credi card debt: https://www.nerdwallet.com/blog/average-credit-card-debt-household/

3. $400: https://www.federalreserve.gov/publications/files/2017-report-economic-well-being-us-households-201805.pdf

4. No retirement savings: https://smartasset.com/retirement/average-retirement-savings-are-you-normal

5. $95,776: https://www.epi.org/publication/retirement-in-america/

6. $5,000: https://www.epi.org/publication/retirement-in-america/

7. 72% of adults: http://www.apa.org/news/press/releases/2015/02/money-stress.aspx

8. Second leading cause: https://www.businesswire.com/news/home/20180207005698/en/Money-Ruining-Marriages-America

9. 59% of workers: https://www.aboutschwab.com/modernwealth2019

10. Federal Reserve report: https://www.federalreserve.gov/publications/files/2017-report-economic-well-being-us-households-201805.pdf

11. 12 million people: https://www.finder.com/payday-loans-statistics

Chapter 1: None

Chapter 2

1. Cornell Study: https://news.cornell.edu/stories/2014/09/doing-makes-you-happier-owning-even-buying

Chapter 3:

1. Guy Raz: https://www.npr.org/podcasts/510313/how-i-built-this

2. Golbal Benefits Survey: https://www.forbes.com/sites/nextavenue/2018/12/26/retirement-employers-just-dont-get-it/#9e1264127345

3. CFPB reports: https://www.marketwatch.com/story/many-employers-are-clueless-about-retirement-2019-01-10?siteid=rss&rss=1

4. 16% of workers: https://www.bls.gov/opub/ted/2018/51-percent-of-private-industry-workers-had-access-to-only-defined-contribution-retirement-plans-march-2018.htm

5. Wages have remained stagnent: https://hbr.org/2017/10/why-wages-arent-growing-in-america

6. 33.4% of workers: http://thehill.com/homenews/state-watch/326995-census-more-americans-have-college-degrees-than-ever-before

7. Age Progression Study: https://www.ncbi.nlm.nih.gov/pmc/articles/PMC3949005/

Chapter 4:

1. Franklin Mint: https://www.investmentnews.com/gallery/20120702/FREE/702009999/PH/10-collectibles-that-werent-worth-collecting

2. Trinity study: https://www.forbes.com/sites/wadepfau/2018/01/16/the-trinity-study-and-portfolio-success-rates-updated-to-2018/#4f4ae0646860

3. Michigan Study: https://www.ncbi.nlm.nih.gov/pubmed/24637231

4. Loss of $6 trillion: https://www.wsj.com/articles/another-recession-is-looming-1538088367

5. Beanie Babies: http://www.thefiscaltimes.com/2015/03/02/How-Great-Beanie-Baby-Bubble-Went-Bust

6. Census data $127,200: https://www.census.gov/const/uspriceann.pdf

7. Toyota Corolla 1987: https://www.cargurus.com/Cars/1987-Toyota-Corolla-Trims-c4172

8. Per capital income: https://united-states.reaproject.org/analysis/comparative-trends-analysis/per_capita_personal_income/tools/0/0/

9. Census data: https://www.census.gov/construction/nrs/pdf/uspricemon.pdf

10. Toyotal Corolla 2017: https://www.kbb.com/toyota/corolla/2017/

11. Compounidng Interest Albert Einstein: https://www.cbsnews.com/news/compound-interest-the-most-powerful-force-in-the-universe/

Chapter 5: None

Chapter 6:

1. $1.4 million: https://www.aboutschwab.com/modern-wealth-index-2018

2. $2.3 million: https://www.aboutschwab.com/modernwealth2019

3. Schwab Modern Wealth Index: https://www.aboutschwab.com/modern-

wealth-index-2018

4. Millionaires: https://finance.yahoo.com/news/woman-studied-600-millionaires-found-110049408.html

5. World Gallup Poll: https://www.marketwatch.com/story/this-is-exactly-how-much-money-you-need-to-be-truly-happy-earning-more-wont-help-2018-02-14

6.Fidelity Investments: https://www.marketwatch.com/story/the-dark-reason-so-many-millennials-are-miserable-and-broke-2019-05-13

7. 25 minutes: https://project.wnyc.org/commute-times-us/embed.html#5.00/42.000/-89.500

Chapter 7

1. BLS $74,644: https://www.bls.gov/opub/reports/consumer-expenditures/2016/home.htm

2. BLS definition of income: https://www.bls.gov/opub/btn/volume-6/use-with-caution-interpreting-consumer-expenditure-income-group-data.htm?view_full#_edn1

3. $10,489: https://www.bls.gov/cex/2016/combined/region.pdf

4. $6,863: https://www.fool.com/retirement/2018/04/29/how-does-the-average-american-spend-their-paycheck.aspx

Chapter 8

1. Nerdwallet: https://www.nerdwallet.com/blog/loans/total-cost-owning-car/

2. ASPCA estimates: https://www.moneyunder30.com/the-true-cost-of-pet-ownership

Chapter 9

1. Credit card debt Nerdwallet: https://www.nerdwallet.com/blog/average-credit-card-debt-household/

Chapter 10

1. SHED data: https://www.federalreserve.gov/publications/files/2017-report-economic-well-being-us-households-201805.pdf

2. Payscales: https://www.payscale.com/college-roi

3. Money magazine: http://time.com/money/5259908/public-college-salaries-roi-payscale-2018/

4. 213%: https://trends.collegeboard.org/sites/default/files/2017-trends-in-college-pricing_0.pdf

5. $50,000: https://www.cnbc.com/2017/11/29/how-much-college-tuition-has-increased-from-1988-to-2018.html

6. $1.5 trillion: https://www.nerdwallet.com/blog/average-credit-card-debt-household/

7. Nerdwallet $46,822: https://www.nerdwallet.com/blog/average-credit-card-debt-household/

8. Law school debt $112,776: https://www.nerdwallet.com/blog/average-credit-card-debt-household/

9. 44%: http://www.newyorkfed.org/research/current_issues/ci20-1.pdf

Chapter 11

1. ProPublica: https://www.propublica.org/article/older-workers-united-states-pushed-out-of-work-forced-retirement

2. Gallup Poll: https://www.cbsnews.com/news/why-so-many-americans-hate-their-jobs/

Chapter 12

1. Shark Tank: https://www.imdb.com/title/tt1452445/quotes

2. Colin Powell quote: https://quotepark.com/quotes/1921662-colin-powell-capital-is-a-coward-it-flees-from-corruption-and/

Chapter 13: None

Chapter 14

1. 14.54% Treasuries: https://www.nytimes.com/1981/08/08/business/treasury-bill-rate-at-14.54.html

2. State of Illinois: http://www.chicagotribune.com/business/columnists/ct-illinois-chicago-municipal-bonds-junk-0611-biz-20170609-story.html

3. 11% CD rates: https://www.bankrate.com/banking/cds/historical-cd-interest-rates-1984-2016/

4. Nerdwallet: https://www.nerdwallet.com/blog/investing/millennial-retirement-fees-one-percent-half-million-savings-impact/

Chapter 15: None

Chapter 16

1. Investment Calculator: https://smartasset.com/investing/investment-calculator

Chapter 17

1. Fortune 500: https://www.planadviser.com/retirement-industry-people-moves-february-16-to-march-2-2018/

2. 40 Credits Social Security: https://eligibility.com/social-security

3. Calculator: https://www.ssa.gov/oact/quickcalc/early_late.html

4. Forecasts: https://www.ssa.gov/oact/tr/2017/tr2017.pdf

5. Life expectancy: https://www.statista.com/statistics/274513/life-expectancy-in-north-america/

6. Congressional pensions: https://www.investopedia.com/articles/markets/080416/how-congress-retirement-pay-compares-overall-average.asp

7. Trustees report: https://www.ssa.gov/OACT/tr/2017/tr2017.pdf

Chapter 18

1. NBER study: http://www.nber.org/papers/w24489

2. E-myth animated: https://www.youtube.com/watch?v=rixrWUI3Nzc

3. 20% profitable: https://www.foxbusiness.com/features/six-alternative-investments-for-fat-returns

Chapter 19

1. Uber $100,000 https://blogs.wsj.com/digits/2013/11/25/uber-cuts-deals-to-lower-car-costs/

2. Economic Policy Index: https://www.epi.org/publication/uber-and-the-labor-market-uber-drivers-compensation-wages-and-the-scale-of-uber-and-the-gig-economy/

3. Economic Policy Indes: https://www.epi.org/publication/uber-and-the-labor-market-uber-drivers-compensation-wages-and-the-scale-of-uber-and-the-gig-economy/

Chapter 20: None

Chapter 21: None

Chapter 22: None

Chapter 23

1. How the Economic Machine Works: https://www.youtube.com/watch?v=PHe0bXAIuk0

2. $33 trillion: https://www.nytimes.com/2018/04/09/us/politics/federal-deficit-tax-cuts-spending-trump.html

Chapter 24: None

Chapter 25

1. Adequate sleep: https://www.mayoclinic.org/healthy-lifestyle/adult-health/in-depth/sleep-the-foundation-for-healthy-habits/art-20270117

2. May Clinic: https://www.mayoclinic.org/healthy-lifestyle/fitness/in-depth/interval-training/art-20044588

3. $285,000 for health care: https://www.cnbc.com/2019/04/02/health-care-costs-for-retirees-climb-to-285000.html

4. 1,000 people: https://www.usatoday.com/story/money/personalfinance/retirement/2018/04/20/retiree-couples-face-medical-bills-280000-dollars/534438002/

Chapter 26

1. Wes Moss: https://www.wesmoss.com/news/why-its-critical-to-find-your-core-pursuits-before-retirement/

2. $36.5 billion: https://www.bloomberg.com/news/features/2018-05-03/america-s-elderly-are-losing-37-billion-a-year-to-fraud?utm_campaign=news&utm_medium=bd&utm_source=applenews

3. 60 percent of cases: https://www.bloomberg.com/news/features/2018-05-03/america-s-elderly-are-losing-37-billion-a-year-to-fraud?utm_campaign=news&utm_medium=bd&utm_source=applenews

Available on Amazon or LoadedforLife.com

BECOME LOADED FOR LIFE!

10 STAGES WORKBOOK

BY NATE CARTER

FINANCIAL INDEPENDENCE

RETIRING EARLY

MAXIMIZING HAPPINESS

Made in the USA
Las Vegas, NV
01 May 2021

22341206R00152